seven methods of killing kylie jenner

Jasmine Lee-Jones

methuen | drama

LONDON • NEW YORK • OXFORD • NEW DELHI • SYDNEY

METHUEN DRAMA
Bloomsbury Publishing Plc
50 Bedford Square, London, WC1B 3DP, UK
1385 Broadway, New York, NY 10018, USA
29 Earlsfort Terrace, Dublin 2, Ireland

BLOOMSBURY, METHUEN DRAMA and the Methuen Drama logo are
trademarks of Bloomsbury Publishing Plc

First published in Great Britain by Oberon Books 2019
This edition published by Methuen Drama 2021
Copyright © Jasmine Lee-Jones, 2019, 2021

Cover image © Niall McDiarmid

A catalogue record for this book is available from the British Library.

A catalog record for this book is available from the Library of Congress.

ISBN: PB: 978-1-350-27748-9
ePDF: 978-1-350-27749-6

Series: Modern Plays

Printed and bound in Great Britain

To find out more about our authors and books visit
www.bloomsbury.com and sign up for our newsletters.

THE ROYAL COURT THEATRE PRESENTS

seven methods of killing kylie jenner

by Jasmine Lee-Jones

seven methods of killing kylie jenner was part of the Royal Court's Jerwood New Playwrights programme, supported by Jerwood Arts.

seven methods of killing kylie jenner was first performed at the Royal Court Jerwood Theatre Upstairs, Sloane Square, on Thursday 04 July 2019, and at the Jerwood Theatre Downstairs on Wednesday 16 June 2021.

seven methods of killing kylie jenner
by Jasmine Lee-Jones

CAST (in alphabetical order)

Kara **Tia Bannon**
Cleo **Leanne Henlon**

Director **Milli Bhatia**
Designer **Rajha Shakiry**
Co-Lighting Designers **Jessica Hung Han Yun, Amy Mae**
Sound Designer **Elena Peña**
Movement Director **Delphine Gaborit**
Assistant Director **Shereen Hamilton**
Associate Designer **Jemima Robinson**
Voice & Dialect **Hazel Holder, Eleanor Manners**
Therapeutic Associate **Wabriya King**
Stage Managers **Constance Oak, Mica Taylor**
Deputy Stage Manager **Sylvia Darkwa Ohemeng**
Set built by **Ridiculous Solutions**
Tree sculpture made by **Syeda Bukhari, Ella Callow**
Scenic Artist **Alice Collie**

From the Royal Court, on this production

Casting Director **Amy Ball**
Company Manager **Joni Carter**
Stage Supervisor **Steve Evans**
Lead Producer **Chris James**
Sound Supervisor **Emily Legg**
Production Manager **Marius Rønning**
Lighting Supervisor **Eimante Rukaite**
Costume Supervisor **Lucy Walshaw**

seven methods of killing kylie jenner
by Jasmine Lee-Jones

Jasmine Lee-Jones (Writer)

For the Royal Court: **Living Newspaper, seven methods of killing kylie jenner, dark matter (Beyond the Court), say her name, drinking concrete [co-writer] (Open Court).**

As writer, other theatre includes: **My White Best Friend (and Other Letters Left Unsaid) (Bunker).**

As performer, theatre includes: **The Last Days of Judas Iscariot (Guildhall); The Reluctant Fundamentalist (Yard/Finborough); Dido Queen of Carthage, The Malcontent (Globe Young Players).**

As writer/performer, theatre includes: **I Used to Love H.E.R. (Atlantic Theater Company).**

As performer, film includes: **Pink [short].**

Awards include: **Evening Standard Award for Most Promising Playwright, Alfred Fagon Award, Stage Debut Award for Best Writer, Critics' Circle Theatre Award for Most Promising Playwright, European New Talent Drama Award (seven methods of killing kylie jenner).**

Jasmine was a writer-on-attachment for the 2016 Open Court Festival.

Tia Bannon (Kara)

For the Royal Court: **seven methods of killing kylie jenner.**

Other theatre includes: **Dead Don't Floss [part of New Views] (National); The Winter's Tale, Pericles (Globe); Camelot: Shining City (Sheffield Theatres).**

Television includes: **Midsomer Murders, This is a Relationship, Shakespeare & Hathaway.**

Film includes: **The Midnight Sky, Drifters, Balls [short], Nightless [short], Oxygen & Terror [short].**

Radio includes: **Camberwell Green, Pygmalion, Martians, Relativity 2.**

Milli Bhatia (Director)

As director, for the Royal Court: **Living Newspaper, seven methods of killing kylie jenner, My White Best Friend (and Other Letters Left Unsaid), This Liquid Earth: A Eulogy in Verse [Edinburgh International Festival], Half Full (& RWCMD), Dismantle This Room.**

As assistant director, for the Royal Court: **Inside Bitch (& Clean Break), Poet in da Corner, One For Sorrow, Instructions for Correct Assembly, Girls & Boys.**

As director, other theatre includes: **Dismantle This Room, The Hijabi Monologues (Bush), My White Best Friend (and Other Letters Left Unsaid) (Bunker), Empower House (Theatre Royal, Stratford East).**

As director, film includes: **HOME(BODY) or The Tall Story (Young Vic), Yash Gill's Power Half Hour, Tiny Dancers (NYT).**

As director, audio includes: **Ghosts In The Blood (Audible).**

Milli is a Literary Associate at the Royal Court.

Delphine Gaborit
(Movement Director)

For the Royal Court: **Living Newspaper, Scenes with girls, seven methods of killing kylie jenner.**

Other theatre includes: **The Suicide (National); Way Up Stream (Chichester Festival).**

As associate movement director, theatre includes: **Pinocchio (National); The Curious Incident of the Dog in the Night-Time (National & International tours); Harry Potter and the Cursed Child (West End).**

As movement coach, film includes: **First Song [short], Wild Rose, Tell It to the Bees, The Titan.**

Delphine trained as a dancer and has been working as a performer for 20 years with choreographers in the UK and across Europe. In 2009 she started a nine year collaboration with Sasha Waltz and Guests in Berlin, joining the company for seven creations touring all over the world. As a movement director, Delphine has worked across theatre, film and visual art. She has collaborated and toured with artists such as Martin Creed for *Ballet 1020*, Adam Linder for his Choreographic Service No.1, *Some Cleaning*, and Anthea Hamilton for *The Squash*, her Duveen Galleries commission at Tate Britain in 2018 and *Cabbage Four Ways* at the Walker Museum, Minneapolis in 2021.

Shereen Hamilton
(Assistant Director)

For the Royal Court: **seven methods of killing kylie jenner.**

As director, theatre includes: **Jamie Hale: CRIPtic Pit Party (Barbican).**

As co-director & producer, theatre includes: **Bitchcraft (Tristan Bates/John Thaw Studio/Melanin Box Festival); Blacktress (John Thaw Studio).**

As assistant producer, theatre includes: **London South Bank Director Theatre Showcase, Evolution Festival (Lyric, Hammersmith).**

As assistant producer, film includes: **Bars.**

Shereen has previously worked as a stage manager and production manager.

Leanne Henlon (Cleo)

seven methods of killing kylie jenner is Leanne's professional debut.

Hazel Holder (Voice & Dialect)

For the Royal Court: **Ear for Eye, Poet in Da Corner, Grimly Handsome, Pigs & Dogs, Father Comes Home from the Wars (Parts 1, 2 & 3).**

Other theatre includes: **Death of England: Delroy, Death of England, Small Island, Nine Night, Barber Shop Chronicles, Pericles, Angels in America, Les Blancs, Ma Rainey's Black Bottom (National); Uncle Vanya, Death of a Salesman (& Young Vic), Dreamgirls [as resident director] (West End); Pass Over (Kiln); Richard II (Sam Wannamaker).**

Television includes: **The Power, In the Long Run, Kate & Koji, Poldark.**

Film includes: **Small Axe, Silent Twins, Death on the Nile.**

Jessica Hung Han Yun
(Co-Lighting Designer)

For the Royal Court: **Living Newspaper, seven methods of killing kylie jenner, Pah-La.**

Other theatre includes: **Blindness (Donmar/UK Tour/ Royal Theater Carré, Amsterdam/Daryl Roth, New York); Inside (Orange Tree); The Band Plays On (Crucible); Dick Whittington (National); Fairview (Young Vic); Equus (Theatre Royal, Stratford East/ETT/Trafalgar Studios/UK Tour); Snowflake (Kiln); The Last of the Pelican Daughters (Complicité, Edinburgh/Royal & Derngate); Cuckoo (Soho); Armadillo (Yard); Rockets & Blue Lights (Royal Exchange Theatre, Manchester); Reasons to Stay Alive (Sheffield Theatres/ETT/UK Tour); One (HOME/UK Tour/ International Tour); Summer Rolls (& Bristol Old Vic), A Pupil (Park); Faces in the Crowd, Mephisto [A Rhapsody], Dear Elizabeth, The Human Voice (Gate); Forgotten (Moongate/New Earth/Arcola/Theatre Royal, Plymouth); Hive City Legacy (Hot Brown Honey/Roundhouse); Nine Foot Nine (Bunker/Edinburgh Festival Fringe); Becoming Shades (VAULT Festival).**

Awards include: **Knight of Illumination Award for Plays, Off West End Award – Best Lighting Design (Equus).**

Amy Mae
(Co-Lighting Designer)

Theatre includes: **Half Breed (Talawa/Soho/ Edinburgh Festival Fringe); The Playboy of the Western World (Gaiety, Ayr/Market Place & Arts Centre, Armagh/Lyric, Belfast); There Are No Beginnings (Leeds Playhouse); Two Trains Running (Royal & Derngate/ETT/RTST); Noises Off (Lyric, Hammersmith); The Memory of Water (Nottingham Playhouse); The Trick (Bush/UK Tour); Start Swimming (& Edinburgh Festival Fringe), Wild East (Young Vic); Hansel & Gretel (Rose); The Fisherman (New Perspectives/ Edinburgh Festival Fringe/Arcola/West End/ UK Tour); Three Sat Under The Banyan Tree (Polka/Belgrade, Coventry/UK Tour); About Leo (Jermyn Street); Mountains: The Dreams of Lily Kwok (Royal Exchange, Manchester/ UK Tour); Br'er Cotton (Theatre503); Othello, Jeckyll & Hyde (NYT); The Host (Yard/St. James Church, Piccadilly); The Ugly One (Park); Babette's Feast (Print Room); I'm Not Here Right Now (& Paines Plough), The Lounge (Soho); Wordsworth (Theatre By The Lake); Paradise Of The Assassins (Tara Arts); Knife Edge (Pond Restaurant, Dalston); Minaturists 55 (Arcola); Prize Fights, Henry V (RADA); Orphans (Southwark); Macbeth (Italia Conti); Liola (New Diorama); Children in Uniform, Punk Rock (Tristan Bates); The Three Sisters (Cockpit); Sweeney Todd (Harrington's Pie & Mash Shop/ West End/Barrow, New York); Pool, The Gut Girls (Jack Studio).**

Dance includes: **Sense of Time (Royal Ballet, Birmingham); The Legacy (The Place).**

Circus includes: **The Exploded Circus (Pavilion, Worthing/UK Tour).**

Awards include: **Knight of Illumination (Sweeney Todd).**

Eleanor Manners (Voice & Dialect)

Theatre includes: **Othello (NYT); Searching for the Heart of Leeds, Dinner 18:55 (Leeds Playhouse).**

Elena Peña (Sound Designer)

For the Royal Court: **Living Newspaper, seven methods of killing kylie jenner.**

Other theatre includes: **Open Mic (ETT & Soho); Women of Troy (LAMDA); Rockets & Blue Lights, Macbeth, Mountains (Royal Exchange, Manchester); Autoreverse (BAC); Boat (& BAC), Brainstorm (& National), Everything (Company Three); Snowflake, The Kilburn Passion, Arabian Nights (Kiln); Misty (& West End), Going Through, Hir, Islands (Bush); The Memory of Water (Nottingham Playhouse); The Remains of the Day (Out of Joint/Royal & Derngate, Northampton); Thick As Thieves (Clean Break); The Wizard of Oz (Pitlochry Festival); All of Me (China Plate); Double Vision (Wales Millennium Centre); The Caretaker (Bristol Old Vic); The Lounge (Soho/ Summer Hall, Edinburgh); How I Hacked My Way Into Space (Unlimited/UK tour); Years of Sunlight (Theatre503); The Bear/The Proposal, Flashes (Young Vic); Sleepless (Analogue/ Staatstheater Mainz, Germany); The Christians (& Traverse), I Call My Brothers, The Iphigenia Quartet, Unbroken (Gate); Thebes Land, Ant Street, Brimstone & Treacle, Knives In Hens (Arcola); You Have Been Upgraded (Unlimited/ Science Museum); Seochon Odyssey (HiSeoul Festival, Korea); Mass Observation (Almeida).**

Dance includes: **Patrias, Quimeras (Sadlers Wells/ Paco Peña Flamenco Company).**

Television/online includes: **Have Your Circumstances Changed?, Brainstorm, The Astro Science Challenge.**

Radio includes: **Rockets & Blue Lights, The Meet Cute, Twelve Years, Duchamps Urinal.**

Installation includes: **Have Your Circumstances Changed?, Yes These Eyes Are The Windows (ArtAngel).**

Awards include: **Offie On Comm Award for Best Audio Production (Rockets & Blue Lights).**

Elena is an Associate Artist for Inspector Sands.

Jemima Robinson
(Associate Designer)

As designer, theatre includes: **Everything (Company Three); Frankenstein (Inside Out Theatre, Beijing); Oedipus at Colonus (Cambridge Arts); I'll Take You To Mrs Cole (Complicite/Polka); Whitewash (Soho); The Trick (Bush/UK Tour); Keith?, New Nigerians, Thebes Land, Maria de Buenos Aires (Arcola); Twelfth Night (Guangzhou Dramatic Arts Centre, China/RSC); Hansel & Gretel (Opera for Hidden Woods, Ilford Arts); Br'er Cotton, The Dark Room (Theatre503); Twist (Theatre Centre); The Majority (National); We Too, Are Giants, Almost But Not Quite, Invisible Boy (Kiln/Mapping Brent Festival); DYL, Sparks (Old Red Lion); Licence to Ill, This Will End Badly, Little Malcolm & His Struggle Against (Southwark); Animal Farm,**

The Bacchae (St George's College); Parallel Yerma (Young Vic); Hearing Things (Albany); I Love You, You're Perfect, Now Change (Zorlu Centre); Dark Vanilla Jungle (& Arcola), Enemy of the People (& Tour), Water's Edge (Talimhane, Istanbul); The Tempest (Watermill); Synergies: NEBT (Sadler's Wells); Aliens (Alma Tavern); Love's Labour (Lost Circomedia, Bristol); Pride & Prejudice (Bristol Old Vic).

As designer, opera includes: **Bierdermann & the Arsonists (Sadler's Wells).**

Awards include: **Max Rayne Bursary, Independent Opera Award (Bierdermann & the Arsonists), Linbury Award (The Tempest).**

Rajha Shakiry (Designer)

For the Royal Court: **seven methods of killing kylie jenner.**

Other theatre includes: **Return of Danton (Collective Ma'louba, Germany); Autoreverse (BAC); Richard II (Globe); Misty (& West End), Going Through (Bush); The Dark (Fuel); Nine Night (& West End), Master Harold & the Boys (National); The Mountaintop (Young Vic/UK tour); Muhammad Ali & Me (Albany/UK tour); Mobile (Paper Birds); How Nigeria Became (Unicorn); Sweet Taboo (Embassy); I Stand Corrected (Artscape/Ovalhouse); Richard II (Ashtar/Hisham's Palace/Jericho/Globe); Still Life Dreaming (Pleasance, Edinburgh); Safe (New Diorama); The Lion & the Unicorn (Eastern Angles); Krunch (National Arts Festival, Grahamstown); Speak (Albany/Rich Mix); Moj of the Antartic (Lyric, Hammersmith/ Ovalhouse/South Africa tour); Visible (Contact, Manchester/Liverpool Everyman/Ustinov, Bath/Soho); Everything is Illuminated; Nymphs & Shepherds (Ectetera); Goblin Market (Sydmonton Festival/Southwark); The Ghost Downstairs [co-designer] (New Perspectives); The Wall, Changes (Cardboard Citizens).**

Dance includes: **Head Wrap Diaries (The Place); Power Games (Jerwood Dance, Ipswich/ Edinburgh Festival Fringe).**

Opera includes: **Don Giovanni, Le Nozze Di Figaro (St Andrew's Church/Beauforthuis, Netherlands).**

Rajha's work was exhibited at the V&A's *Make:Believe* Exhibition.

THE ROYAL COURT THEATRE

The Royal Court Theatre is the writers' theatre. It is a leading force in world theatre for cultivating and supporting writers – undiscovered, emerging and established.

Through the writers, the Royal Court is at the forefront of creating restless, alert, provocative theatre about now. We open our doors to the unheard voices and free thinkers that, through their writing, change our way of seeing.

Over 120,000 people visit the Royal Court in Sloane Square, London, each year and many thousands more see our work elsewhere through transfers to the West End and New York, UK and international tours, digital platforms, our residencies across London, and our site-specific work. Through all our work we strive to inspire audiences and influence future writers with radical thinking and provocative discussion.

The Royal Court's extensive development activity encompasses a diverse range of writers and artists and includes an ongoing programme of writers' attachments, readings, workshops and playwriting groups. Twenty years of the International Department's pioneering work around the world means the Royal Court has relationships with writers on every continent.

Since 1956 we have commissioned and produced hundreds of writers, from John Osborne to Jasmine Lee-Jones. Royal Court plays from every decade are now performed on stage and taught in classrooms and universities across the globe.

We're now working to the future and are committed to becoming carbon net zero and ensuring we are a just, equitable, transparent and ethical cultural space - from our anti-oppression work, to our relationship with freelancers, to credible climate pledges.

It is because of this commitment to the writer and our future that we believe there is no more important theatre in the world than the Royal Court.

Find out more at royalcourttheatre.com

JERWOOD
ARTS

Jerwood New Playwrights is a longstanding partnership between Jerwood Arts and the Royal Court. From 1994 until 2019, Jerwood New Playwrights supported the production of two new plays by emerging writers in the Jerwood Theatres Upstairs and Downstairs. In 2020, the partnership pivoted to focus on commissioning writers earlier in their creative journey enabling them to nurture and develop an idea, supported by the Royal Court team. Through the Jerwood Development Fund, the Royal Court offers facilitated workshops, readings and other development opportunities for early-career writers, enabling them to select the resources needed to hone their craft.

The Royal Court carefully identifies playwrights whose careers would benefit from the challenge and profile of being selected as a Jerwood New Playwright.

Since 1994, the programme has produced a collection of challenging and outspoken works, which explore a variety of new forms and voices, and so far has supported the production of 86 new plays. These plays include: Joe Penhall's **Some Voices**, Nick Grosso's **Peaches** and **Real Classy Affair**, Judy Upton's **Ashes and Sand**, Sarah Kane's **Blasted**, **Cleansed** and **4.48 Psychosis**, Michael Wynne's **The Knocky** and **The People Are Friendly**, Judith Johnson's **Uganda**, Sebastian Barry's **The Steward of Christendom**, Jez Butterworth's **Mojo**, Mark Ravenhill's **Shopping and Fucking**, Ayub Khan Din's **East Is East** and **Notes on Falling Leaves**, Martin McDonagh's **The Beauty Queen of Leenane**, Jess Walters' **Cockroach, Who?**, Tamantha Hammerschlag's **Backpay**, Connor McPherson's **The Weir**, Meredith Oakes' **Faith**, Rebecca Prichard's **Fair Game**, Roy Williams' **Lift Off**, **Clubland** and **Fallout**, Richard Bean's **Toast** and **Under the Whaleback**, Gary Mitchell's **Trust** and **The Force of Change**, Mick Mahoney's **Sacred Heart** and **Food Chain**, Marina Carr's **On Raftery's Hill**, David Eldridge's **Under the Blue Sky** and **Incomplete and Random Acts of Kindness**, David Harrower's **Presence**, Simon Stephens' **Herons**, **Country Music** and **Motortown**, Leo Butler's **Redundant** and **Lucky Dog**, Enda Walsh's **Bedbound**, David Greig's **Outlying Islands**,

Zinnie Harris' **Nightingale and Chase**, Grae Cleugh's **Fucking Games**, Rona Munro's **Iron**, Ché Walker's **Fleshwound**, Laura Wade's **Breathing Corpses**, debbie tucker green's **Stoning Mary**, Gregory Burke's **On Tour**, Stella Feehily's **O Go My Man**, Simon Faquhar's **Rainbow Kiss**, April de Angelis, Stella Feehily, Tanika Gupta, Chloe Moss and Laura Wade's **Catch**, Polly Stenham's **That Face** and **Tusk Tusk**, Mike Bartlett's **My Child**, Fiona Evans' **Scarborough**, Levi David Addai's **Oxford Street**, Bola Agbaje's **Gone Too Far!** and **Off the Endz**, Alexi Kaye Campbell's **The Pride**, Alia Bano's **Shades**, Tim Crouch's **The Author**, DC Moore's **The Empire**, Anya Reiss' **Spur of the Moment** and **The Acid Test**, Penelope Skinner's **The Village Bike**, Rachel De-lahay's **The Westbridge** and **Routes**, Nick Payne's **Constellations**, Vivienne Franzmann's **The Witness** and **Pests**, E. V. Crowe's **Hero**, Anders Lustgarten's **If You Don't Let Us Dream, We Won't Let You Sleep**, Suhayla El-Bushra's **Pigeons**, Clare Lizzimore's **Mint**, Alistair McDowall's **Talk Show**, Rory Mullarkey's **The Wolf from the Door**, Molly Davies' **God Bless the Child**, Diana Nneka Atuona's **Liberian Girl**, Cordelia Lynn's **Lela & Co**, Nicola Wilson's **Plaques and Tangles**, Stef Smith's **Human Animals**, Charlene James' **Cuttin' It**, Nathaniel Martello-White's **Torn**, Alice Birch's **Anatomy of a Suicide**, Chris Thorpe's **Victory Condition**, Simon Longman's **Gundog**, Ellie Kendrick's **Hole**, Eve Leigh's **Midnight Movie** and Jasmine Lee-Jones' **seven methods of killing kylie jenner.**

The Royal Court and Jerwood Arts continue to work together in proud partnership to support the voices of emerging writers.

Jerwood Arts is the leading independent funder dedicated to supporting UK artists, curators and producers to develop and thrive. It enables transformative opportunities for individuals across art forms, supporting imaginative awards, fellowships, programmes, commissions and collaborations. It presents new work and brings people from across the arts together in the galleries at Jerwood Space, London, as well as across the UK and online.

jerwoodarts.org

COMING UP AT THE ROYAL COURT

17–28 Aug
THE SONG PROJECT
Some things can only be sung
THE SONG PROJECT began as a bold experiment bringing together a group of artists and playwrights to co-create in a new way, starting with the idea that some things can only be sung.

Conceived by Royal Court associate designer and award-winning Dutch singer and composer **Wende**, in collaboration with composer **Isobel Waller-Bridge**, choreographer **Imogen Knight**, and playwrights **E.V. Crowe**, **Sabrina Mahfouz**, **Somalia Nonyé Seaton**, **Stef Smith** and **Debris Stevenson**.

10 Sep–23 Oct
IS GOD IS
By **Aleshea Harris**
Aleshea Harris' award-winning play collides the ancient, the modern, the tragic, the spaghetti Western, hip-hop and Afropunk. This revenge tale about two women seeking justice and taking control of their own narratives has received the Obie Award for Playwriting.

29 Sep–23 Oct
WHAT IF IF ONLY
A new short play by **Caryl Churchill**
Your partner's died, could things have been different? Caryl Churchill's recent work includes GLASS. KILL. BLUEBEARD. IMP. and ESCAPED ALONE. Many of her plays which first premiered at the Royal Court are now considered modern classics including TOP GIRLS, A NUMBER and FAR AWAY.

10 Nov–18 Dec
RARE EARTH METTLE
By **Al Smith**
Al Smith's epic new play is a brutally comic exploration of risk, delusion and power. Three worlds collide on a Bolivian salt flat - a British doctor, a Silicon Valley billionaire and the indigenous community meet. Each pursue their own ambitions, but which is the greatest good?

RARE EARTH METTLE has been generously supported with a lead gift from Charles Holloway. Further support has been received from the Cockayne Grant for the Arts, a donor advised fund of The London Community Foundation. This play is a recipient of an Edgerton Foundation New Play Award.

ASSISTED PERFORMANCES

Captioned Performances

Captioned performances are accessible for people who are D/deaf, deafened & hard of hearing, as well as being suitable for people for whom English is not a first language.

seven methods of killing kylie jenner: Wed 30 June, Wed 7 July, Wed 14 July, 7.45pm
The Song Project: Fri 27 Aug, 8pm
Is God Is: Wed 6 Oct, Wed 13 Oct, Wed 20 Oct, 7.30pm
What If If Only: Wed 13 Oct, Wed 20 Oct, 6pm
Rare Earth Mettle: Wed 1 Dec, Wed 8 Dec, Wed 15 Dec, 7.30pm

Audio-described Performances

Audio-described performances are accessible for people who are blind or partially sighted. They are preceded by a touch tour which allows patrons access to elements of theatre design including set and costume.

The Song Project: Pre-show notes available for all performances from Mon 23 Aug
Is God Is: Sat 23 Oct, 3pm
What If If Only: Sat 23 Oct, 6pm
Rare Earth Mettle: Sat 11 Dec, 2.30pm

ROYAL

ASSISTED PERFORMANCES

Performances in a Relaxed Environment

Relaxed Environment performances are suitable for those who may benefit from a more relaxed environment.

During these performances:
- There is a relaxed attitude to noise in the auditorium; you are welcome to respond to the show in whatever way feels natural
- You can enter and exit the auditorium when needed
- We will help you find the best seats for your experience
- House lights remain raised slightly
- Loud noises may be reduced

seven methods of killing kylie jenner: Sat 24 July, 3.30pm
Is God Is: Sat 16 Oct, 3pm
What If If Only: Sat 16 Oct, 6pm
Rare Earth Mettle: Sat 4 Dec, 2.30pm

If you would like to talk to us about your access requirements, please contact our Box Office at (0)20 7565 5000 or boxoffice@royalcourttheatre.com
The Royal Court Visual Story is available on our website. We also produce Story and Sensory synopses which are available on request.

COURT

ROYAL COURT SUPPORTERS

The Royal Court relies on its supporters every year in addition to our core grant from Arts Council England and our ticket sales. 2020 was an unusual year in so many ways and we are particularly grateful to the individuals, trusts and companies who stood by us and continued to support our work during these difficult times. It is with this vital support that the Royal Court remains the writers' theatre and that we can continue to seek out, develop and nurture new voices, both on and off our stages.

Thank you to all who support the Royal Court in this way. We really can't do it without you.

PUBLIC FUNDING

ARTS COUNCIL ENGLAND
Supported using public funding by

CHARITABLE PARTNERS

JERWOOD ARTS

BackstageTrust

ORANGE TREE TRUST

CORPORATE SPONSORS

Aqua Financial Ltd
Cadogan
Colbert
Edwardian Hotels, London
Kirkland & Ellis International LLP
Kudos

CORPORATE MEMBERS

Platinum
Auriens
Bloomberg Philanthropies

Gold
Weil, Gotshal & Manges (London) LLP

Silver
Kekst CNC
Left Bank Pictures
Patrizia
Sloane Stanley

TRUSTS & FOUNDATIONS

The Derrill Allatt Foundation
The Backstage Trust
Martin Bowley Charitable Trust
CHK Foundation
The City Bridge Trust
The Cleopatra Trust
Cockayne – Grants for the Arts
The Noël Coward Foundation
Cowley Charitable Foundation
The D'Oyly Carte Charitable Trust
Edgerton Foundation
The Golden Bottle Trust
Roderick & Elizabeth Jack
Jerwood Arts
The London Community Foundation
John Lyon's Charity
Claire McIntyre's Bursary
Old Possum's Practical Trust
Lady Antonia Fraser for the Pinter Commission
The Richard Radcliffe Charitable Trust
Rose Foundation
The Charles Skey Charitable Trust
The Sobell Foundation
John Thaw Foundation
The Garfield Weston Foundation

To find out more about supporting the Royal Court please get in touch with the Development Team at support@royalcourttheatre.com, call 020 7565 5049 or visit royalcourttheatre.com/support-us

Royal Court Theatre
Sloane Square,
London SW1W 8AS
Tel: 020 7565 5050
info@royalcourttheatre.com
www.royalcourttheatre.com

Artistic Director
Vicky Featherstone
Executive Producer
Lucy Davies

Associate Directors
Ola Ince*, Lucy Morrison, Hamish Pirie, Sam Pritchard (International)
Associate Designer
Chloe Lamford*
Trainee Directors
Philip Morris, Izzy Rabey

General Manager
Catherine Thornborrow
Producer
Chris James
International Producer
Daniel Kok
Producing Co-ordinator
(maternity leave)
Tanya Follett
Producing Co-ordinator
(maternity cover)
Sharon John
Assistant to the Artistic Director & Executive Producer
Romina Leiva Ahearne

Head of Participation
Vishni Velada Billson
Participation Manager
Romana Flello
Participation Co-ordinator
Vicky Berry*
Participation Facilitator
Ellie Fulcher*
Participation Engagement Officer
Jasmyn Fisher-Ryner*

Literary Manager
Jane Fallowfield
Literary Associates
Milli Bhatia*, Ellie Horne, Myah Jeffers

Casting Director
Amy Ball
Casting Co-ordinator
Arthur Carrington

Head of Production
Marius Rønning
Production Manager
Simon Evans
Company Manager
Joni Carter^
Head of Lighting
Johnny Wilson
Deputy Head of Lighting
Matthew Harding
Lighting Technicians
Cat Roberts, Eimante Rukaite, Stephen Settle
Head of Stage
Steve Evans
Deputy Head of Stage
TJ Chappell-Meade
Stage Show Technician
Ben Carmichael
Head of Sound
David McSeveney
Deputy Head of Sound
Emily Legg
Head of Costume
Lucy Walshaw
Deputy Head of Costume
Katie Price

Finance Director
Helen Perryer
Financial Controller
Edward Hales
Accounts Assistant
Anais Pedron*
Finance & Administration Assistant
Annie Moohan

Head of Press & Publicity
Anoushka Warden
Press Assistant
Rosie Evans-Hill

Head of Marketing & Sales
Holly Conneely
Sales & Ticketing Manager
Farrar Hornby
Marketing Officer (Digital)
Joanne Stewart
Audience Development Co-ordinator
Moni Onojeruo
Box Office Sales Assistants
Katherine Hearst*, Caitlin McEwan*, Tiffany Murphy*, Felix Pilgrim*, Jade Sharp*

Development Director
Vicki Grace
Deputy Development Director
Charlotte Christesen
Development Manager
Charlotte Cole
Development Officer
Sarah Bryce

Theatre Manager
Rachel Dudley
Deputy Theatre Manager
Harvey Dhadda
Duty House Managers
Jess Andrews*, Tristan Rogers*, Sydney Stevenson*
General Maintenance Technician
David Brown

Bar & Kitchen Manager
Robert Smael
Bar & Kitchen Supervisors
Jemma Angell*, Lauren Dickson*, Stephen Hamilton*, Milla Tikkanen*

Stage Door
Paul Lovegrove, Fiona Sagar*

Manager of Samuel French Bookshop at the Royal Court Theatre
Simon Ellison
Bookshop Assistant
Terry McCormack*

Thanks to all of our Ushers and Bar & Kitchen staff.

^ The post of Company Manager is supported by Charles Holloway.

* Part-time.

ENGLISH STAGE COMPANY

President
Dame Joan Plowright CBE

Honorary Council
Sir Richard Eyre CBE
Alan Grieve CBE
Joyce Hytner OBE
Phyllida Lloyd CBE
Martin Paisner CBE

Council Chairman
Anthony Burton CBE
Vice Chairman
Graham Devlin CBE
Members
Jennette Arnold OBE
Judy Daish
Noma Dumezweni
Pamela Jikiemi
Mwenya Kawesha
Emma Marsh
James Midgley
Winsome Pinnock
Andrew Rodger
Anita Scott
Lord Stewart Wood
Mahdi Yahya

BAR & KITCHEN

The Royal Court's Bar & Kitchen aims to create a welcoming and inspiring environment with a style and ethos that reflects the work we put on stage. Alongside our vibrant basement bar, you can visit our pop-up outdoor bar Court in the Square throughout summer 2021.

Offering expertly crafted cocktails alongside an extensive selection of craft gins and beers, wine and soft drinks, the Royal Court bars provide a sanctuary in the middle of Sloane Square. By day a perfect spot for meetings or quiet reflection and by night atmospheric meeting spaces for cast, crew, audiences and the general public.

All profits go directly to supporting the work of the Royal Court theatre, cultivating and supporting writers – undiscovered, emerging and established.

For more information, visit
royalcourttheatre.com/bar

HIRES & EVENTS

The Royal Court is available to hire for celebrations, rehearsals, meetings, filming, ceremonies and much more. Our two theatre spaces can be hired for conferences and showcases, and the building is a unique venue for bespoke weddings and receptions.

For more information, visit
royalcourttheatre.com/events

Sloane Square London, SW1W 8AS ⊖ Sloane Square ⇌ Victoria Station
🐦 royalcourt 📘 theroyalcourttheatre 📷 royalcourttheatre

Support the Court

Be a part of our future by donating to our Support the Court fund, with every penny raised going directly towards producing bold new writing for our stages, cultivating and supporting writers in the UK and all over the world, and inspiring the next generation of theatre-makers through our programmes for young people.

Donate today to #SupportTheCourt and be a part of our story.

Text 70560 5 to donate £5

Text 70560 10 to donate £10

Text 70560 20 to donate £20

Texts cost the donation amount plus one standard message. UK networks only.

Or to find out more about the different ways in which you can get involved, visit our website: royalcourttheatre.com/support-us

seven methods of killing kylie jenner

PPLDEM

CLEO a.k.a. **@INCOGNEGRO** on Twitter,
Black* dark(er)-skinned woman, 21,
smart and dope as fuck but also hella problematic

KARA, Black* mixed-race woman, 22,
alpha female but also vulnerable

VOICES OF THE TWITTERSPHERE
(I recommend they be voiced and characterised
by the two actors playing **CLEO** and **KARA**, but it
might work with more actors or in another way)

**Political blackness isn't a thing, but if it ever was
it certainly isn't in this play.*

NOTES ON THE TWITTERSPHERE

The tweets seen in the play are merely a cross-section of
the tweets that come about as a result of @INCOGNEGRO's
methods; they are the ones that affect and encroach upon their
world the most. Memes and gifs are part of the world of Twitter
and so they are part of the world of this play. This meme is a
good summation of the whole play and the characters of **CLEO**
and **KARA** respectively:

It's up to the creatives and actors of each production how the
Twittersphere is realised and embodied but however it is done
the most important thing is that it's <u>specific</u>.

Over the course of the play, the Twittersphere begins to infect
and encroach upon their space. Twitter language like *tbh* and
wtf should be read out letter-by-letter; *LOL* should be read
phonetically especially in its elongated form *LOOOOOOOL*.
Both performers should also find a way to embody and give
voice to emojis like 🦷 and 🐱 both on the TL and IRL (even this
instruction should be read out as such 😛). When the language
they are using IRL resembles that of the Twittersphere, it could
be said that **CLEO** and **KARA** are glitching – make of that
what you will…

NOTES ON THE ANATOMY

Sections occurring on Twitter are labelled with TWITTERLUDE, sections occurring in real life are titled IRL.

There are two parts of The Premeditation: Part I, which is optional, and Part II which is compulsory. Part I is a proposed way to recontextualise the production in a time other than 2019 and Part II is a flashforward or teaser and is re-contextualised in The Post-Mortem.

BIG UP

Rachel De-Lahay
Somalia Seaton
debbie tucker green
Rajha Shakiry
Jane Fallowfield
Tia Bannon
Danielle Vitalis
Hamish Pirie
Vicky Featherstone
Martin Derbyshire
Jennifer Thomas
Araba Aduah
Grace Akinbode
Jade Anouka
Leah Harvey
Alice Birch
Alistair McDowall
Ellie Fulcher
Ella Saunders
Serena Grasso
Shereen Hamilton
Sylvia Darkwa-Ohemeng
Everyone at the Royal Court
The Osei-Tutus

The amazing Milli Bhatia for your bottomless belief, patience and work during this process

Everyone who made *seven methods* happen in some way, shape or form

My family, especially Mum and Dad: love you to the moon and back

And finally, all the unnamed black womxn and gender-nonconforming people whose spirits and souls have infused and imbued my life and now my work.

Bless up!

"Now, it is not addressed particularly to white people, though it does not put you down in any way: it simply ignores you. For my people need all the inspiration and love that they can get…"

– To Be Young Gifted and Black,
Nina Simone, *Black Gold* (1970)

"Thinking ahead of time
Why don't you spend the night?
I know you love me…"

– Hold On, The Internet (2017)

THE PREMEDITATION

I.

Silence.

And darkness.

Even more darkness.

A sound like an engine starting. Subtle whirring at first, but then undeniable as it grows in volume and density. Like a volcano about to erupt or a rocket launching or a bullet train raring to go at full speed.

Suddenly: it's take-off and we realise we are on a rollercoaster of sorts, back through the shitstorm of the last two years. Back to the Future *type shit. Or should I say* Black to the Future*. A time machine in reverse chronological order.*

It should start with the most recent news updates. Should feel hot off the press as of the day of the performance. Could be live updated during the run of the play. As of the beginning of May, when this play went into rehearsal, the most recent updates included:

Chatter of roadmaps and lifting lockdowns. The Israel and Palestine conflict.

Then we go further back in time, and the net of news and current affairs widens. We hear of assault allegations, abuses of power, mayoral elections, some school in South banning natural hairstyles. Soundbites of the Meghan and Harry interview. Oprah asking if Meghan was 'siLENT' or 'siLENCED'. The sound of women shouting 'We will not be silenced' and the name Sarah Everard.

The time machine amps up a notch and we're going at lightning speed.

We hear the sound of Biden being inaugurated and Kamala whimpering, 'We did it Joe!' Shouts from the storming of the Capitol. Chants from choruses of crowds shouting 'Stop Asian Hate'. Then Trump blowing his own trumpet during the presidential debate with Joe Biden. News of Indian farmers' strikes.

1

Then the name George Floyd is heard. And 'Black Lives Matter! Black Lives Matter! Black Lives Matter!' Then other chants: 'No Justice, No Peace, No Racist Police!' 'Say Her Name!' 'ACAB!' And more names: Ahmaud Arbery, Rayshard Brooks. So many names. An accent or emphasis on the names of Black female bodies: Breonna Taylor. Nicole Smallman. Bibaa Henry. Toyin Salau. Belly Mujinga. Shukri Abdi.

The echo of heavy statues being pulled down. Shouts of glory.

Then we're almost blinded by a proliferation of Black squares. Then chatter of COVID. How it disproportionately affects Black bodies. Then back to the beginnings of the pandemic. Conspiracy theories mixed with cold fact. Emergency service sirens sound and circle blue and red.

Suddenly we are plunged back into a deep darkness and landed in a different present.

THE PREMEDITATION

II.

Early morning. Outside. A park. Dark.

KARA and CLEO drag something resembling a body across a park. Suddenly they approach a hole. They look into the hole and then throw whatever they were dragging in. Cover it with a bit of earth.

They stand over the hole. Maybe wipe their hands.

Blackout.

1.

The past.
A couple of hours before.
5th March 2019. 4:01AM.
The bird expands and suddenly we are on Twitter.
A few birds are heard tweeting in a tree. Then one sings loud and clear.

 Forbes
@Forbes

At 21, Kylie Jenner becomes the youngest self-made billionaire ever
#ForbesBillionaires

04:01 AM - 5 Mar 2019

♡ ⟲ ♡ ✉

A fracas of retweeting, quote tweeting, liking and following commences. Like locusts reproducing. Then, breaking through the fracas, @INCOGNEGRO tweets.

INCOGNEGRO
@INCOGNEGRO

YT woman born into rich American family, somehow against all odds, manages to get more rich......

04:15 AM - 5 Mar 2019

♡ ⟲ ♡ ✉

INCOGNEGRO @INCOGNEGRO · Mar 5

Errybody and they aunty need to quit fronting like Kylie killing it! She ain't killing shit! And tbh if I had it my way the only thing getting kilt would be that bitch! #kyliejennerfidead

🗨 ↻ ♡ ✉

(Retweet) (Like) (Retweet) (Like)

INCOGNEGRO @INCOGNEGRO · Mar 5

Yep das right! I said it! Kylie Jenner can gwarn and get deaded!

🗨 ↻ ♡ ✉

(Retweet) (Follow) (Like)

INCOGNEGRO @INCOGNEGRO · Mar 5

And how exactly does one kill a social media figure/entrepreneur or as I like to term her a con artist-cum-provocateur?
A THREAD

🗨 ↻ ♡ ✉

(Like) (Retweet) (Like)

INCOGNEGRO
@INCOGNEGRO

METHOD #1
#DEATHBYPOISON
Kinda like the temporary lip fillers that helped you gain
Acclaim
For bringing fuller lips into fashion

04:24 AM - 5 Mar 2019

🗨 ↻ ♡ ✉

INCOGNEGRO
@INCOGNEGRO

But when Mac instagrammed a picture of a Black model with lips of the same width
She was called ugly
Defiled
Reviled
While you are profiled by Vogue
Elle
A daily story on Snapchat

04:27 AM · 5 Mar 2019

♡   ⇅   ♡   ☒

INCOGNEGRO
@INCOGNEGRO

METHOD #2
#DEATHBYSHOOTING

04:32 AM · 5 Mar 2019

♡   ⇅   ♡   ☒

INCOGNEGRO @INCOGNEGRO · Mar 5
Now I'm not talking about shoots of the photo kind
I'm talking about the ones that will get her left behind
In the middle of the road with ten warning shots to her chest
The kind of shoots that will have her name on a sign in a protest

♡   ⇅   ♡   ☒

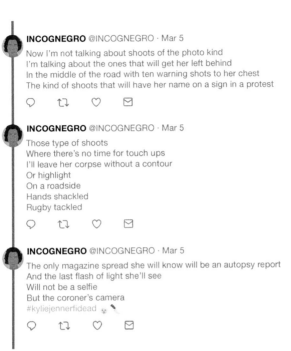

INCOGNEGRO @INCOGNEGRO · Mar 5

Now I'm not talking about shoots of the photo kind
I'm talking about the ones that will get her left behind
In the middle of the road with ten warning shots to her chest
The kind of shoots that will have her name on a sign in a protest

INCOGNEGRO @INCOGNEGRO · Mar 5

Those type of shoots
Where there's no time for touch ups
I'll leave her corpse without a contour
Or highlight
On a roadside
Hands shackled
Rugby tackled

INCOGNEGRO @INCOGNEGRO · Mar 5

The only magazine spread she will know will be an autopsy report
And the last flash of light she'll see
Will not be a selfie
But the coroner's camera
#kyliejennerfidead

Suddenly a figure enters lurking. She creeps on CLEO; touches her.

CLEO jumps.

KARA: *(In a roadman lilt.)* Fuck are you on blad!

Suddenly the IRL environment is illuminated and we realise we are in CLEO's room. We see both girls in the flesh. CLEO in her inside clothes – she looks disgusting and magnificent – and KARA in her outside clothes – she looks casually hawt like she hasn't tried but still very peng I can't lie.

CLEO: Kara?

KARA is creasing.

Fucksake Kara man! Shit! How many times have I told you you can't just sneak into my yard like this?

KARA: How many times have I told you to fix that damn window? It's been mash since we were 17! We do live in ends you know.

Beat.

Ay big man ting why does it smell like crotch in here?

CLEO: Big man ting why couldn't you just text me if you wanted to come over like a regular person instead of doing up hoodrat shit.

KARA: Well I would text you but you've been airing my Whatsapps consistently for four days now.

CLEO: What are you even doing up at this time?

KARA: Well if you *must* know, I was at one of my lovers' houses –

CLEO: Oh lord. Which bitch is it this time?

KARA: Scuse me! Can you not refer to my lovers as bitches please? I'd much prefer you use the gender-nonspecific term: tings.

CLEO: Oh my god.

KARA: Anyway so I'm lying there post-nut and I swear to God I felt my chakras come out of line. It was sooooooo visceral like that time I made spiritual contact with Prince –

CLEO: – you mean when you were *high* –

KARA: – when I made spiritual contact with Prince… It was like that but eeeeeeeven stronger cus it was you and you're living and you're my bredrin. I could just feel something was up with you. Then I rolled over, picked up my phone to bell man only to see you on a Bin Laden flex on the TL.

CLEO: Oh my days…

KARA: Don't "oh my days" me. Wahum with you?

CLEO: Wahum? Wahum? Wahum is I see a wildly incorrect tweet disgrace my TL alluding to a certain someone born into the limelight born into instantaneous wealth being categorised as a self-made billionaire. *Self*-made…*SELF*-MADE! She's about as self-made as my bed.

KARA: See why couldn't you just tweet that. A simple intelligent disagreement with a dose of wit. Like you usually do on that account. Nuanced. No killings. No knife emojis. Nobody haffi dead.

CLEO: Listen yeah the other day I handed in an essay about the effects of colonialism on the black female form and I'd been working on it for weeks night and day! Cited all my sources dem. And the only reason I got marked down is because my professor thought my work didn't show two sides of the argument. Two sides. To slavery! White people be wilin'.

KARA: Look man I'm just tryna stop you from catching a case.

CLEO: Oh my daze you're actually so dramatic. I beg you just let me be vex in peace.

KARA: Let you be vex in peace? Pleeeeeeeeease. That's an oxymoron. Moron.

CLEO: Look it's two-two tweets that helped me vent my frustrations. It's really not that deep…

TWITTERLUDE 1

▬▬▬▬▬▬
@▬▬▬▬▬▬

OMG this bish tryna kill Kylie 🤣 🤣 🤣

04:44 AM - 5 Mar 2019

◯ ⇄ ♡ ✉

Retweet

▬▬▬▬▬▬ @▬▬▬▬▬▬ · Mar 5

I bet this is just another angry black bitch hiding behind a computer screen…
You know what this is really mean? Like what did Kylie do to her

◯ ⇄ ♡ ✉

Retweet Quote Like

▬▬▬▬▬▬ @▬▬▬▬▬▬ · Mar 5

watisdemeaningofalldisjackie

◯ ⇄ ♡ ✉

▬▬▬▬▬▬ @▬▬▬▬▬▬ · Mar 5

So now #woketwitter are putting the world on blast on the TL AND IRL too

◯ ⇄ ♡ ✉

▬▬▬▬▬▬ @▬▬▬▬▬▬ · Mar 5

I'm dedddddddddddddddddddddddddddddddddddddddddddddddddddd

◯ ⇄ ♡ ✉

▆▆▆▆▆▆ @▆▆▆▆▆▆▆ · Mar 5

so is Kylie boo!

💬   🔁   ♡   ✉

Report

▆▆▆▆▆▆ @▆▆▆▆▆▆▆ · Mar 5

YO is @KylieJenner still with us?

💬   🔁   ♡   ✉

▆▆▆▆▆▆ @▆▆▆▆▆▆▆ · Mar 5

I'm criiiiiiiiiiiine.

💬   🔁   ♡   ✉

▆▆▆▆▆▆ @▆▆▆▆▆▆▆ · Mar 5

LOL.

💬   🔁   ♡   ✉

▆▆▆▆▆▆ @▆▆▆▆▆▆▆ · Mar 5

So is @INCOGNEGRO taking assassination requests or nah???

💬   🔁   ♡   ✉

▆▆▆▆▆▆ @▆▆▆▆▆▆▆ · Mar 5

If so can she add my landlord to her list?
#landlordsfideadtoo

💬   🔁   ♡   ✉

▆▆▆▆▆▆ @▆▆▆▆▆▆▆ · Mar 5

Assassination plots I thought we left those in the 60's

💬   🔁   ♡   ✉

████████████ @████████ · Mar 5

Don't y'all know what season this is? this ain't winter it's put a cap in that ass season 😂 😂 😂 😂 😂 😂 😂

♡ ⟲ ♡ ✉

████████████ @████████ · Mar 5

I'm
screeeeeeeeeeeeeeeeeeeeeeeeeeeeeeeeeeeeeeeeeeeeeeeeeeeeeeeeaming

♡ ⟲ ♡ ✉

████████████ @████████ · Mar 5

Kylie when @INCOGNEGRO roll up to her yard

♡ ⟲ ♡ ✉

████████████ @████████ · Mar 5

HAAAAAAAAAAAAAAAAAAAAAAAAAAAAAAAAAAAAAAAAAAA Kylie when @INCOGNEGRO enter the premises
U ready to fucking die!
I'm a bad bitch you can't kill meh!

♡ ⟲ ♡ ✉

████████████ @████████ · Mar 5

SKSKSKSKSKSKSKSKSKSKSKSKSKSKSKRT when @INCOGNEGRO draws for the strap (a la Big Shaq)
The ting go skraaaaa pa pa pa pa pa skiddy dip pa pa and a pum pum pum pum

♡ ⟲ ♡ ✉

████████████ @████████ · Mar 5

OMG I'm weak

♡ ⟲ ♡ ✉

████████████ @████████ · Mar 5

.@INCOGNEGRO when she finished the deed
(a la Denzel) KING KONG AIN'T GOT SHIT ON ME!

♡ ⟲ ♡ ✉

@▨▨▨▨▨▨▨▨▨ · Mar 5

WOOOOOOOOOOOOOOOW y'all rlly kno how to make a bitch kiki! 😂 😂 😂 😂 😂 😂

💬 🔁 ♡ ✉

@▨▨▨▨▨▨▨▨▨ · Mar 5

💬 🔁 ♡ ✉

@▨▨▨▨▨▨▨▨▨ · Mar 5

This thread is gooooooooooooooooooooooooold FFS

💬 🔁 ♡ ✉

RETWEET
LIKE
FOLLOW
LIKE
REPORT
UNFOLLOW
QUOTE TWEET
OMG
OMG
OMG

IRL

KARA kikis a little. Then subsides into total laughter at the tweets.

CLEO: Wooooooooooow. You're actually kiking at all of this? Cool.

KARA: Come on. That last one was kinda funny still.

CLEO: No it weren't.

KARA: Yoooooooooo! Do you reckon they're gonna interview me for women who kill?

CLEO: Wait…what?

KARA: *(Interviewer voice.)* When did you know Cleo was…different?

(Own voice.) Well…to be honest the suspicions all started after what she did to Baby Annabel doll.

CLEO just looks at her.

CLEO: You think you're funny don't you?

KARA: *(Hamming it on.)* Baby Annabel doll was my favourite doll growing up. My prized possession…she was like a child to me and… *(Holding back tears.)* One day when I left the room to play an innocent game of hide and seek. I returned to find Cleo had torn the doll to pieces. And no matter how much I tried…I just couldn't put her back together –

CLEO: You really need to stop smoking hash.

KARA: – it was then I knew she had violent instincts towards white women. As a mixed-race woman myself I often worried she would turn on me…

CLEO: – okay now you're taking the piss –

KARA: *(Interviewer voice.)* As with many serial killers Cleo's childhood exploits were merely a simulation of her later crimes. Practise. Premeditation.

CLEO: Behave.

KARA: *Cleo Fuller: The Black Ted Bundy*. Every Tuesday on The Crime Network.

CLEO: Alright! Why does everything on the TL have to turn into a joke?

KARA: You're lucky no one's taking this seriously.

CLEO: At what point did I indicate I didn't want people to take this seriously?

KARA: Oh please! You knew what you were doing when you posted that tweet. And a whole hashtag too! And I know you wouldn't be moving this mad if the account wasn't anonymous.

CLEO: I'm moving mad? No I'll tell you what's moving mad: that fucking 'self-made billionaire' tweet. Don't you understand? Inside that tweet is hundreds of years of anti-blackness, positive affirmations of capitalism, cultural appropriation… In under fifty characters it colludes in the systematic historical and present-day dehumanization of the black female body and the buttressing and idolatry of white womanhood in abusive hegemonic white infrastructures.

KARA: I'm not gonna lie I don't understand a word of what you just said.

CLEO: I said –

KARA: Just speak English, not…dissertation.

CLEO: I'm just saying I read about this shit constantly. Throughout history. And then I see it now. Black bodies being used, abused then appropriated by white people. Them profiting off of our pain. It's just. It's just so fucking jarring.

KARA: I mean I hear what you're saying. But it is just a tweet…

CLEO: Just a tweet? Just a tweet? *(À la Chris Tucker.)* Do you understand the words that are coming out of my mouth?

KARA: Yeah I do but –

CLEO: You know what? Say nada. If you man think that was funny it's calm cah I ain't even finished yet.

KARA: What do you mean you ain't –

CLEO: See me nuh.

TWITTERLUDE 2

INCOGNEGRO
@INCOGNEGRO

It seems some of y'all think I'm fucking around!!! Tht's calm cah tbh I ain't even started yet...

04:59 - 5 Mar 2019

♡   ⟲   ♡   ✉

INCOGNEGRO
@INCOGNEGRO

METHOD #3
#DEATHBYDROWNING
I want Kylie to be stuck sunk
Like the 3,000 refugees
Left submerged in the traffic
Of a modern day
Middle passage
Left scrambling
Starving
scratching the surface
For air
Stop her swimming in images of
herself
And her wealth.

05:03 AM - 5 Mar 2019

♡   ⟲   ♡   ✉

████████████

@████████████

Oh shit this bitch acc ain't finished!

05:04 AM - 5 Mar 2019

♡ ↻ ♡ ✉

Retweet

████████ @████████ · Mar 5

Yep she acc crazy and tht's the real tea!

♡ ↻ ♡ ✉

Quote

████████ @████████ · Mar 5

Real talk @INCOGNEGRO just a salty ass heffa who need to get her own shit together

♡ ↻ ♡ ✉

████████ @████████ · Mar 5

Ikr! this whole thread got me feeling like...

♡ ↻ ♡ ✉

Retweet

■■■■■■■■■ @■■■■■■■ · Mar 5

real talk

is any of this rlly tht deep? all kylie done did is inject some fillers into her lips den make some makeup and sell it...dazzit

◯ ⇄ ♡ ✉

Retweet **Like**

■■■■■■ @■■■■■■ · Mar 5

I don't know why @INCOGNEGRO upset Kylie was born rich Kylie whole FAMILY rich even they kids already rich and now you saying you wanna kill her cos of it?!?!?!?!? You know what - y'all SJW kill ME.

◯ ⇄ ♡ ✉

Quote **Like**

■■■■■■■ @■■■■■■■ · Mar 5

Hey @INCOGNEGRO quick QT can ur freedom struggle extend to more than deading YT women pls?

◯ ⇄ ♡ ✉

Retweet

■■■■■■■■■ @■■■■■■■ · Mar 5

Trust me! Little black boys getting kilt in the streets outchea and this is the shit you be riding for?

◯ ⇄ ♡ ✉

Report

▆▆▆▆ ▆▆▆▆▆ @▆▆▆▆▆▆▆▆▆ · Mar 5
Trust me @INCOGNEGRO

Y'ALL FINISHED
OR Y'ALL DONE

♡ ⟲ ♡ ✉

Report

▆▆▆▆▆ ▆▆▆▆▆ @▆▆▆▆▆▆▆▆▆ · Mar 5
.@INCOGNEGRO just outchea ignoring real injustices like…
I cannot see I'm legally blind!

♡ ⟲ ♡ ✉

▆▆▆▆▆ ▆▆▆▆▆ @▆▆▆▆▆▆▆▆▆ · Mar 5
I for one can't believe @INCOGNEGRO acting like dis. U ain't the next
civil rights activist!

♡ ⟲ ♡ ✉

Retweet   Report   Like

▆▆▆▆▆ @▆▆▆▆▆▆ · Mar 5
Right like BIIIIIIIIIIIIIIIIIIIIIIIIITCH THIS AIN'T THE 60'S

♡ ⟲ ♡ ✉

▆▆▆▆▆▆▆▆ @▆▆▆▆▆▆ · Mar 5
Tbh MLK's most probs looking down from heaven like wahum fi dat
gyal deh!

♡ ⟲ ♡ ✉

Retweet

▆▆▆▆▆ @▆▆▆▆▆▆ · Mar 5
Truuuuuuuuuuuu what would he say to all this shit?

♡ ⟲ ♡ ✉

I have a feeling it would sound something like this… "Darkness cannot drive out darkness, only light can do that. Hate cannot drive out hate; only love can do that."

♡   ⟲   ♡   ✉

IRL

KARA: True say I never thought of it like that.

CLEO: You're still taking the piss…right?

KARA: No…think about it it's like…a yin and yang ting innit. Two negative energy forces cannot coexist or move in a forward direction it's basic physics.

CLEO: How is telling the truth putting out negativity into the world?

KARA: Well there's telling the truth and then there's threatening to kill people…two semi-different tings…

CLEO: Oh please. You know there's levels to my shit.

KARA: Yes I do. But all I'm saying to you is think of the ancestors and how they dealt with tings. Tings that were ten times worse than this. MLK dealt with tings with dignity. Never exacted the violence of his oppression on his oppressors.

CLEO: Fuck dignity and fuck MLK! Why is it every time a black person wants to critique something in a non-palatable way motherfucking MLK gets brought into the conversation? How am I s'posed to know what he would have thought of it – that nigga dead! And even if he was alive to denounce my politics – do you think I'd care? That nigga was problematic AF! That whole passive resistance singting? Not for me bredrin. And lest we forget he banged out cheating on Coretta. Yep. Black men including MLK been *historically* trash. FAAAAAAAAAAAAAAACTS.

KARA: How are you managing to drag #menaretrash into this? You're acc wilding sis. You're in a relationship with a black man fuck!

CLEO: …was.

KARA: Oh lord. You went on a break again?

CLEO: Yes but for real this time.

KARA: *(Sceptical.)* As in for real for real or –

CLEO: Yes bitch. Really for real. We done.

KARA: By done do you mean done done or like…done?

CLEO: Done. Done as in done.

KARA: Are you sure?

CLEO: Yes I'm sure. We're done. We're finished.

KARA:

CLEO: Can you stop taking the piss? Yes. We've broken up for good. Because he was…he was cheating on me.

KARA: You're lyyyyyyyyyying.

CLEO: Yes bitch. I caught his ass redhanded in some next bitch's DMs and then I scrolled through his likes and realised they musta started following each other June 29th when we were fully out of linking phase. In fact we were exactly three whole months into our relationship! And even tho we only just broke up so technically the bitch just stopped being a sidepiece the bitch is brazenly commenting shit like 'see you later zaddy' underneath his pics! I'm like have some class bitch! I was there first. I *been* there. Have some fucking tact.

Beat.

Not that I've been preeing him.

KARA just looks at her throughout like:

22

KARA: What did he say when you confronted him?

CLEO: Some BS about how I basically forced him to fuck her because I was no longer matching his energy levels. And I was dragging him down with my weight. Fucking up his chakras or some other hotep shit.

KARA: I beg you stop dating brers like this.

CLEO: What? It's not my fault he was cheating on me.

KARA: No shade sis but this isn't the first time shit's ended up this way.

CLEO: Scuse me?

KARA: Come on Cleo. You deffo have a type. They're always the same. Tortured fakedeeps. Always artists. Usually musicians or worse…actors. Nose piercings. Baby dreads. Tattoos of scriptures from when they used to be Christian. Daddy issues. And the last two have been Pisces when you know say you're a Leo so why do you love off the water signs? Like venture out bredrin. Diversify to rass. Stop dating Daniel Caesar rejects.

CLEO: Excuse you…

KARA: I'm being serious. As a homosexual I live out my occasional heterosexual fantasies through you and you never fail to disappoint.

CLEO: Whatever. All I know is that nigga ain't shit…and I miss him.

KARA: Just let that man go sis. He doesn't deserve you.

CLEO: It's not that…

KARA: Not that what?

CLEO: You wouldn't understand…

KARA: Try me.

Pause.

CLEO: I'm craving dick.

KARA: Craving dick? *(A la Joanne the Scammer.)* Never heard of that…never smelt that…don't know what that is.

CLEO: This is why I don't feel comfortable sharing with you more time. This isn't a friendship free of judgement.

KARA: I'm just joking. I did used to sleep with men you know…

CLEO: Oh please. You ain't sucked dick since twenty-fifteen.

KARA: Alright! No need to call me out by name.

CLEO: Dick withdrawal symptoms are fully kicking in. And I don't get it either cos his dickgame weren't even all that. It was mediocre at best.

KARA: Swear? What was his headgame like?

CLEO: …I wouldn't know…

KARA: This bredda never even ate the box? How is that even a thing? You straight women are wiiiiiiiiild!

CLEO: I know. I know. But it was like it didn't even matter because we were so spiritually connected. I don't know what to do…I'm mad conflicted.

KARA: Buy yourself a vibrator like the rest of us and gwarn.

CLEO: I've tried that, it's not working.

KARA: Buy new batteries then. Cheapskate.

CLEO: Not my vibrator. Wanking in general.

KARA: *(On her own planet.)* Is the word wanking gender-neutral?

CLEO: Masturbation! Whatever! Can we get back on topic? I can do it but I can't…

KARA: What?

CLEO: You know…

KARA: I know…what?

CLEO: Cum! Alright! I can't cum!

KARA: You can't…you've never…

CLEO: I mean yeah I have but not of my own accord. On my ones.

KARA: Are you being serious?

CLEO: Well I did once but…

KARA: …but what?

CLEO: And this is the tea sis. It's only cos I was saying his name as I was doing it. Like I did when we used to beat.

KARA: Hoh. My. GOD. That's actually mad. I ain't never heard shit like that before. He must have put a hex on you or something. Wait. Ohmygod. How could I forget…he's Nigerian innit?

CLEO nods mournfully like:

KARA: I willingly let my sis fall for a Yoruba demon. Shiiiiiiiit den!

CLEO: And that's not even the top of the tea sis.

KARA: There's more?

CLEO: Yep.

KARA: OMG. Spill it please. I'm thirsty.

CLEO: His new ting's a Klan member.

KARA: Wait…what?

CLEO: She's from Mount Caucasus.

KARA: Come again.

CLEO: She's a caucasoid.

KARA: I –

CLEO: Bitch. The bitch is white. She's white.

KARA: I am fully dead.

CLEO: I know I still can't believe the extent of the fuckery. Cah fam if I ever showed the girl. If I eeeeeeeeeeeeever showed you the girl. In her DP she's wearing so much fake tan she looks like a pigeon in an oil spill. And she has lip fillers. Really big lip fillers. Unnatural like. And guess what her name is on twitter? @brownsugar_. Brown Sugar – as in after the D'Angelo song and I know it's after the D'Angelo song because every 5 minutes she wants to be tweeting about how much she loooooooooooooooooooves neo-soul music and trap and drill and bashment and basically anything black. As if she's deliberately advertising herself as The Down White Girl. And the worst thing of all is I can just imagine her bragging to her little white friends about her new bae's big black dick which it's not in fact it's a perfectly medium-sized dick which happens to be black. And not that I'm being dick-discriminatory. I'm really not. One size fits all. It's what you do with it that counts. But as aforementioned his dickgame is whack so in fact all she's doing is fetishising him. Colonising his clart. Is he aware of that? Placing her white flag in his black land. So she can brag to the other explorers about her newfoundland. Her newfoundland man. Faaaaaaaaaaaaaaaam. Dazzit.

KARA deeps shit like:

KARA: Rah this is fully making sense yah na…

CLEO: Right? I might have to coin that shit!

KARA: No I mean… Cleo I know you're going through it right now but doing up a Twitter tirade isn't gonna solve anything. Trust me.

CLEO: Wait you think all of those tweets are about –

KARA: I mean I'm just -

CLEO: Do you actually think I'm that basic?

KARA: I didn't say that…

CLEO: You didn't need to. It's calm. I'll just get back to my crazy Twitter tirade!

KARA: You are joking – right?

CLEO: Nope. I'm being for real bitch cus in the words of the high prophet Cardi B formerly known as Belcalis: 'I'm a boss, you a worker bitch, I make bloody moves…'

TWITTERLUDE 3

INCOGNEGRO
@INCOGNEGRO

METHOD #4
#DEATHBYSKINNING
I want Kylie to be flayed alive
I want her skin to be turned into a
disguise
So I can get inside and don her coil
Her culture as a costume
Mimic her race
And walk around for just a day
In whiteface

05:28 AM - 5 Mar 2019

🗨 ⟲ ♡ ✉

▓▓▓▓▓▓▓ @▓▓▓▓▓▓▓ · Mar 5

Ohhhhhhhhh lordt is this bitch incapable of taking a break from a
screeen???

🗨 ⟲ ♡ ✉

▓▓▓▓▓▓▓ @▓▓▓▓▓ · Mar 5

I for one am doing just tht! Tired of this BS!

![Reclaiming my time. Reclaiming my time.][Reclaiming my time. Reclaiming my time.]

🗨 ⟲ ♡ ✉

██████████ @██████ · Mar 5

Maybe @INCOGNEGRO just ill! She prolly just schizo or some shit!

◯   ⇄   ♡   ✉

Quote

██████████ @██████ · Mar 5

IONO wtf wrong w her but I for one am tired of hearing this negro jihadi bullshit

◯   ⇄   ♡   ✉

Unfollow

██████████ @██████ · Mar 5

LEWL negro jihadi shit that's acc peak!!!!!!

◯   ⇄   ♡   ✉

██████████ @██████ · Mar 5

ROFL

◯   ⇄   ♡   ✉

██████████ @██████ · Mar 5

Y'all can kiki all you like but we both know the bitch done took this shit too far tonight!

◯   ⇄   ♡   ✉

██████████ @██████ · Mar 5

I for one say we boycott the bitch #boycottincognegro

◯   ⇄   ♡   ✉

██████████ @██████ · Mar 5

Right I'm finna leave this damn thread in the past like…,

◯   ⇄   ♡   ✉

Unfollow

29

███████ ██████ @████████ · Mar 5
Y'all can unfollow her but idc cah I'm still waiting on the next method in the saga b!

♡   ⟲   ♡   ✉

Quote   Like   Report

██████ @████████ · Mar 5
I'm weeeeeeeeeeeeeeeeeeak

♡   ⟲   ♡   ✉

████ ██████ @████████ · Mar 5
Lewl! I for one am waiting for @INCOGNEGRO to get her comeuppance

♡   ⟲   ♡   ✉

██████ ████ @████████ · Mar 5
Right I bet the bitch is rlly some 48-year-old white man from Ohio

♡   ⟲   ♡   ✉

Retweet   Follow   Like

██████ ██ ████ @████████ · Mar 5
Haaaaaaaaaaaaaaaaaaa y'all are acc killing me #INCOGNEGROTHEYT

♡   ⟲   ♡   ✉

Retweet

██████ ██████ @████████ · Mar 5
All I know is the TL about to drag @INCOGNEGRO and…. (a la Monique) I would like to see it!

♡   ⟲   ♡   ✉

LOOOOOOOOOOOOOOOOL

RETWEET
QUOTE TWEET
LIKE
UNFOLLOW
LIKE

LIKE

LIKE

LIKE

IRL

KARA: I can't believe this.

CLEO: I know right! They think I'm a forty-eight-year-old white man from Ohio! The cheek of it! Why is it even now they're getting credit for everyting! I actually can't.

KARA: Nah Cleo what I was gonna say is I can't believe you're making this sooooo deep!

CLEO: Hol' up. I'm making this deep?

KARA: I'm js you've made your point just stop now! Why are you just continuing to add fuel to fire for no raisin?

CLEO: Wooooooooow. My own bredrin gaslighting me!

KARA: Yooo. Can you stop using polysyllabic words this early in the morning? I'm gonna have to draw for dictionary.com in a minute.

CLEO: Gaslighting. To manipulate someone via psychological means into doubting their own sanity.

KARA: Wtf! Manipulate you? I'm just tryna understand all this! I'm tryna understand you…these methods and ting…killing? I mean…it's just a bit…extreme.

CLEO: Extreme? Oh I'm extreme now I'm an extremist!

KARA: No. I. Cleo come on. I'm js. You have certain. Your politics they're…radical and –

CLEO: Oh I'm an extremist *radical*! Maybe I shouldn't be let out the house in case I radicalise the youths dem! Maybe the government should start a special PREVENT Cleo scheme.

KARA: You know what Cleo I was wrong. You *are* crazy.

CLEO: And there it is. Out it comes. From Mrs Gaslight herself…

KARA: *(Going to leave.)* You know what? I'm done trying with you now. I'm going to my yard.

CLEO: Ah. You know what Kara I take it back! I'm…sorry. It's early in the morning, my brain's not working too good and I almost forgot…you're a lightie.

KARA: What?

CLEO: You're a lightie. Periodt. No tampon.

KARA: What does me being light-skinned have to do with the price of fish?

CLEO: Everyting.

KARA: …I'm not seeing the link.

CLEO: Course you're not. You see what you're suffering from is an acute case of lightie-itis.

KARA: Lightie-i–?

CLEO: Lightie-itis. Primary symptoms include tardiness, laziness and most importantly in regards to our present predicament: partial blindness. Because when tings are soooo cushty for you, it's obvs hard for you to clock how difficult it is for everyone else…

KARA: You do realise you're chatting out your batty crease right now?

CLEO: Am I? Look around Kara. All the BW considered universally beautiful are lighties. Lighties with green eyes. Freckles. Racially ambiguous hunties. Girls who can get into DSTRKT. Girls who shaku on the beat aswel. Manic pixie mixed girls. The love interests. All the girls in the music videos. Think about it: Beyonce, Rihanna, Jorja Smith. Cassie, Aayliah (may she rest in peace), Ashanti, Amerie! Fuck. It's like the music industry just keeps a closet of 100 lighties and when they get bored they just throw another ten out.

KARA: What does any of that have to do with this situation? Or me for that matter? I ain't never had it easy.

CLEO:

KARA: I haven't.

CLEO:

KARA: Can you stop doing tht? Ffs. It's actually very annoying.

CLEO: /Mmmmmmmohmygod –

KARA: I said fucking stop! I haven't had it easy from day and you of all people should know that…

CLEO: I'm not talking about dem tings deh.

KARA: What are you talking about then?

CLEO: Ite so boom: let's do an empirical analysis of our whole lives.

KARA: Is this a science class or summink?

CLEO: Let's start with primary –

KARA: Primary? As in primary school?

CLEO: Yes primary. In primary you were generally considered very peng.

KARA: You're not serious…

CLEO: I'm not on a paedo ting or anything but you were the first girl in our class to have a boyfriend, and even Miss Fitzgerald always said how pretty your hair was, and the only time she came remotely close to commenting on how nice my hair was, was when my Mum straightened it for the Year 5 pictures. Then there was secondary –

KARA: Here we go…

CLEO: On the eve of year 7 I suggest we both straighten our hair, me with Dark and Lovely and you with tongs. It's a ceremonious expression of our ascent into adolescence and trying to be peng. I musta rinsed that ting in and out a good twenty times to get my hair half as straight as yours! And who gets all the compliments the next day? You. Weren't even you're fucking idea mate.

KARA: You're moving mad petty rn –

CLEO: No I'm not! Furthermore, throughout our secondary education we both know every man was on you.

KARA: Well, not every –

CLEO: And you were under every man…

KARA: Wtf does my hoe phase have to do with this?

CLEO: Wtf does ur hoe phase have to do with this? Wtf does ur hoe phase have to do with this? Ask yourself this: Did I ever have a hoe phase? No. Why? Not a lightie.

KARA: That's acc not why! It only started in secondary when my hips came –

CLEO: Bullshit. When your hips came there was a spike –

KARA: – before that everyone was calling me marga Kara

CLEO: Mandem only called you that for bants but you and I both know they were still tryna get you to off-pant.

KARA: Oh and a man wanting to off-pant is the key to black female liberation…

CLEO: Shut up and let me finish! Cah even before the hips came you were considered one of the buffest in the borough. Remember when you dyed your hair blonde and every man and his mum was commenting hotspice, lahhhhhhh, whosdat underneath the pic like there was no tomorrow. You had guys drooling at your feet from before the hips came cos the hips came over the summer of year 10 and you dyed ur hair blonde in the summer of year 9. So don't come to me with some cack about it was when the hips came cus it just wasn't! It just wasn't okay! And even if hypothetically it might have been how come even when
I got hips
when I got batty
I was still getting moved less than you?
Answer that for me one time please

KARA: I mean –

CLEO: Exxxxxxxxxxxxactly!

KARA: So what Cleo? So what I got moved to by more man possibly because I was light-skinned?

CLEO: It means –

KARA: – nuttin. That's what it means. It means – meant fucking around with a hundred multiple mandem my whole youth that I didn't even fucking like. That I didn't even wanna be with. Meant pretending to be someone I'm not half my life. And that wasn't exactly fucking breezy Cleo.

CLEO: Oh please.

KARA: Do you think I wanted man to be watching face constantly? Always moving me just for the sake of it? I never consented to being someone's light-skinned fantasy…cus that's what I was Cleo. That's all I was.

CLEO: But you were still desired. I was discarded. Not even fucking seen to be discarded in the first place. Not even regarded. Constantly in your shadow.

KARA: Do you know how much I would have given to disappear them years? To not be looked at like a fucking lightie trophy wife? More times I'd look at my body in the mirror and feel disgusted. Hate myself for letting multiple man bore tru me like it was nuttin!

CLEO: I'd rather that than being ostracised all the fucking time. Blacklisted. Literally. Definition of the word. Do you remember the typa shit ppl used to call me?

KARA: No actually I don't

CLEO: Course you don't, because you have ligh–

KARA: And it's not because of my lightie-itis or whatever made-up illness all light-skinned people supposedly have! Because guess what I am still a fucking black woman! I am still oppressed! I too know why the caged bird sings! Fuck. You don't own blackness Cleo! You don't own blackness just because you're dark-skinned!

CLEO: I'm not tryna own blackness. I'm telling my truth and truth be told throughout my life I've been shamed for being in my skin… in my body…

KARA: What r u talking about?

CLEO: A little thing I like to call #wiggate…

KARA: #wiggate?

CLEO: The shubz in Year 12…?

KARA: Oh my god. Don't drag that into this –

CLEO: After that night. I'll drag what I want where I like. U kno y? Because u have no idea of my experience. Well maybe an iota but not the full-bodied trauma. It's like you experience racism but it's diluted. Like…you're a cordial or something.

KARA: A cordial?

CLEO: Like a Ribena…Robinsons ting.

KARA: Are you actually being for real right now? Comparing me to Ribena – you might as well be calling me a half-breed! You seem to think your life's been harder than mine but like you said Cleo I used to straighten my hair too! Every morning until it was burnt, broken and damaged within an inch of its life. So bad that I chose to cut it off. Why? Cus I, like you, wanted to be more white and look less black! So why am I now being @'d in this situation? It makes no fucking sense!

CLEO: Oh of course you're finding a way to make this about you. There goes the lightie-itis again.

KARA: I swear to god if you say the word lightie-itis one more time I am going to explode.

CLEO: L–

KARA: I'm not playing with you.

CLEO: Light–

KARA: I swear down!

CLEO: Lightie-ihhhhhh/

KARA: If you don't –

CLEO: /us! Lightie-itus! Lightie-itus! Lightie-itus! Lightie-itus!

KARA: Eurgh you're so! You're so fucking jarring!

CLEO: HAAAAAA!

KARA: You're just a troublemaker! This isn't even about Kylie is it?

CLEO: Yes it is.

KARA: Nah it's not. You just like creating unnecessary passa.

CLEO: No I'm not I'm just tryna demonstrate the truth. It's like you're Kylie and I'm Jordyn –

KARA: That makes no fucking sense.

CLEO: It does. You know it does. Back in the old days I'd be the field nigger out shucking corn and you'd be in the house beating the master.

KARA: WTH is wrong w u rn? A) Slavemasters *raping* and *sexually assaulting* slaves is not 'beating', B) We're not American so the example you're using is general as fuck and C) regardless of where I would have been in the house and where you would have been in the house, we were still stuck in the same fucking house!

CLEO makes a sound like KARA's pressed a wrong button.

CLEO: Wrong! A-gain! *You* would be stuck in the house. Not me. I would have barely even got to touch the house. I would have been sleeping in one cabin outta yard!

KARA: Eurgh you know what I mean! *Enslaved!* We would have both been *slaves!*

CLEO: Me and you are not the same Kara!

KARA: I know we're not – and I for one praise Jah for that!

CLEO: You know what if you don't wanna be involved in my *passa* as you call it – maybe we should just dead this friendship entirely!

KARA: Wait. WHAT!?!

CLEO: *(À la Kanye West.)* Real friends, how many of us?

KARA: BMT why are you behaving like this?

CLEO: BMT why are you talking to me like I'm crazy?

KARA: WTF is wrong with you right now! Are you smoking dick or something? Or is this just a symptom of your dick deprivation?

CLEO: Oh. You think you're funny now! That's calm cus I don't have to sit around listening to any more of this rubbish. I have a thread to finish. So hasta la vista, bon voyage, bonsoir and bye bitch!

TWITTERLUDE 4

INCOGNEGRO
@INCOGNEGRO

METHOD #5
#DEATHBYIMMOLATION
I want Kylie to be burnt
Skin blackened to a crisp
With the meaningless
Fire emojis left under
Her heavily modified
Photoshopped
Cropped selfies
Can you take a selfie whilst being lit
But like actually lit on fire?

05:44 AM - 5 Mar 2019

♡   ⟲   ♡   ✉

━━ @▓▓▓▓▓▓▓ · Mar 5
This incogNIGGER bitch is only jealous of Kylie bcos of how ugly she was
us a pickaninny....

♡   ⟲   ♡   ✉

━━ @▓▓▓▓▓▓▓ · Mar 5
This just in incogNIGGER kept her monkey looks as a teenager too…

> A PICTURE OF AN
> ADOLESCENT MONKEY

♡   ⟲   ♡   ✉

41

███████████ @█████████████ · Mar 5

Glad to see in adulthood incogNIGGER's kept her monkey ways

A PICTURE OF A GORILLA

█████████ @███████████ · Mar 5

😂 😂 😂 😂 😂 😂 😂 😂

███████████ @███████████ · Mar 5

AN IMAGE OF A
BLACK WOMAN
BEING LYNCHED

IRL

KARA: Oh my god this is mad! This is more than mad, this is maaaaaaaaaaad!

CLEO: Calm down.

KARA: Calm down? Calm down? How can I remain calm right now?

KARA begins chanting to soothe herself.

CLEO: What are you doing?

KARA: I'm chanting to bid away the toxicity of this situation.

She carries on with increased intensity.

CLEO: Can you stop doing that it's acc proper scary.

KARA: Proper racists are threatening to rape and kill you on the TL and I'm the one that you find scary!

CLEO begins to laugh.

Y r u laughing? This isn't funny.

CLEO: It's just. You said proper racists…

KARA: You know what I mean! Like redneck racists! *Ruh*-racists! Racists with a capital 'R'!

CLEO: Wooooooooooooooooooooooooooooooooooooooow.

KARA: You need to do something.

CLEO: Like what?

KARA: I don't know!… Report them! Report them to Twitter!

CLEO: What's the point? It's not gonna stop them from making another account. And another one, and… *(Repeatedly.)*

KARA: How are you making jokes out of this rn?

CLEO: Cus this shit's happened to me before. It's calm.

KARA: What? But it's not right. It's. It's. Overt now. It's not a joke ting anymore.

CLEO: Well if it's bothering you so much why don't *u* do something about it?

KARA: Wait what…

CLEO: Since all of a sudden you seem to be sooooo outraged about how I'm being treated on the TL.

KARA: Wait why are you turning this back on me? I was the one who told you to slow your roll in the first place and you carried on tweeting. All of this could have been prevented if you just listened to me.

CLEO: Oh. I'm sorry. I'm sorry. I'm sorry that I didn't let Captain Kara the light-skinned saviour save the day again! I'm sorry. Maybe you could try actually doing something and @ them yourselves! Go on! Tell the 'proper' racists wagwarn.

KARA: Why would I tweet them when I didn't start any of this? You instigating it is your business.

CLEO: Ohhhhhhhh. I see! It's happening to me not you and so it's not your business. I get it now. I get it. Yk what this reminds me of soooooo much? #wiggate.

KARA: *(À la Grand Theft Auto.)* Ow shit here we go again! How many times are you gonna bring this up!

CLEO: As many times as I like cus u still ain't apologised. Not properly anyway.

KARA: We were 16 Cleo can you make like Elsa and let it go! Ffs.

CLEO: U don't get to decide when I let something go.

KARA: Wtf! U can't just live with shit! Ur clearly not over it so let's hash it out! Let's talk about… #wiggate or wotever it is you wanna call it.

CLEO: Why is it always you deciding when we get to speak about something

KARA: OMDS ur soooooooooooooooooooooo long. Just talk! FFS!

CLEO: I'll decide when I'm ready to speak.

KARA:

Long fucking silence.

KARA and CLEO look like two cowboys getting ready for a duel. Think Tombstone or Unforgiven or some other country and western type shit. They are about to fight to the death.

A tumbleweave may cross the stage.

CLEO: I'm ready now.

Fuckery number #1:

I didn't even wanna go to tht shubz in the first place

KARA is taking the piss out of CLEO, either making faces as she speaks or miming along with her speech with her hand like a puppet.

What are you doing?

KARA: Nothing.

CLEO: Fuckery number #2

We were supposed to meet at 9

KARA: 30.

CLEO: 9.

KARA: KMT.

CLEO: Anyways ur black ass or should I say *half*-black ass decides to rock up at 10.

Like say the time we planned to meet was a suggestion!

The time we plan to meet is not a guideline.

KARA: I was busy that day I had shit to do.

CLEO: What?

KARA: IDK this was 5, 6 years ago

#wheniwasstraight

So I was most probs linking my ting at the time which was Andre

Who got us into the party anyway

So that's why I was late

Cos I was linking the person who was gonna get us into the party

So no need to say ty ur welcome.

CLEO: Don't. Even. TRY IT!

If that was the plan all along then why did you tell me 9 and get there at 10?

Ah eediat ting!

10 on the dot.

Like you knew you were gonna be late

Like it was something you pre-planned, to pre-emptively fuck with the timings.

A pre-empted fuckery.

KARA: ...Sorry?

Sorry for being late 5 years ago...

CLEO: Hold your sorries until fuckery #4 pls and thanku

Fuckery #3

U told me tht this party was gonna b calm
That it was for yungas only
And there wasn't gonna b no funny business
So tell me why when we get there there's hotboxes everywhere
Nah scratch that
Just one massive marijuana cloud clogging up everyone's windpipes
And drink everywhere
14-year-olds wining up on 40-year-olds

KARA: You loooooooooooooooove exaggerating

CLEO: Fuckery #4
So we're in the shubz and this man grabs me by the waist and starts daggering me
Ur in the corner kiking as if all of this is a joketing
When you knoooooooooow say –

KARA: You didn't even wanna be there in the first place
Yes.
I know.
FFS
STOP MENTIONING IT!

CLEO: And I'm tryna push this guy off
Cus I didn't consent to his crotch area being near my crotch area
Simulating you know what

KARA:

CLEO: But what do you kno?
He doesn't fucking listen
They never fucking listen
Do they?
And I say no
But he keeps trying it anyway
Then he gets vile
Violent with his words
"Ur butters anyway look at u fam ur blick"
And all his boys start laughing

47

And then another one's like
"LOOOOOOOOOOOL look at her droplip"
as I'm tryna get out
Get to the door
One of them grabs my wig
And it falls clean onto the floor
All I remember is bare laughter
Everyone creasing
Crying
Camera's flashing without my consent
Over and over
Images posted all over socials
Me a meme
A silent, unconsenting gif
Like I was some sort of spectacle
Or a fucking freak
I've never felt so ugly in my life
To this day
Never
And the thing that gets me everytime
When I think about it
Is I *wasn't* on my one's
You were there
And you didn't say jack.
Did you?

KARA is silent.

You didn't help me then and you're not helping me now.
What a surprise!
So go on @ them if you're bad.
@ those racists.
Prove you're not an opp.
Go on.
Tweet something.

KARA: Idk how that would help anything?

CLEO: So you're not doing it?

KARA: Cleo you're being –

CLEO: Okay. Confirmed. SNM. I don't need you anyway. Bun you blad.

TWITTERLUDE 5

 **New York Post**
@nypost

#kyliejennerfidead: Anonymous Twitter Activist under pseudonym @INCOGNEGRO incites violence against Kylie on Twitter

06:01 AM - 5 Mar 2019

Público
@publico_es

La activista social @INCOGNEGRO amenaza con matar a Kylie Jenner en Twitter

06:02 AM - 5 Mar 2019

 **The Guardian**
@guardian

#kyliejennerfidead: Has Social Activism on Twitter Gone Too Far?

06:03 AM - 5 Mar 2019

FRANCE 24
@FRANCE24

Activiste @incognegro provoque une action militante contre Kylie Jenner sur Twitter. #kyliejennerfidead

06:03 AM - 5 Mar 2019

◯ ⇄ ♡ ✉

Fox News
@FoxNews

#kyliejennerfidead: Twitter's new lethal form of social activism

06:06 AM - 5 Mar 2019

◯ ⇄ ♡ ✉

DutchNews.NL
@DutchNewsNL

Is het Twitter activisme te ver gegaan?

06:09 AM - 5 Mar 2019

◯ ⇄ ♡ ✉

CNN
@CNN

#kyliejennerfidead: clickbait or killbait?

06:13 AM - 5 Mar 2019

◯ ⇄ ♡ ✉

IRL

CLEO: Shiiiiit den.

Pause.

KARA: Are you enjoying this?

CLEO: I'm finally being heard.

KARA: Ur acc getting kicks out of this? Ur fully sick in the head.

CLEO: No acc I'm not. There's nothing wrong with me. If there was something wrong with me I wouldn't be being recognised on a worldwide stage for my activism. A bitch about to be verified!

KARA: That's what you're thinking about? About your blue tick… your backseat activism… 'course you are… little miss woke queen…

CLEO: Scuse me?

KARA: I'm just saying.

CLEO: You're just saying what?

KARA: Nothing. Forget it.

CLEO: Nah fam. Say what you said.

KARA: Nothing it's calm.

CLEO: It's clearly not so just say it.

KARA: I'm not tryna get into it with you still so just chill.

CLEO: I'm not tryna get into it with you either I'm just asking you to say what you said with your chest!

KARA: Fine! What I said. I just said. You're not perfect.

CLEO: And –? Neither are you.

KARA: I know but –

CLEO: But what?

KARA: It's just ur gwarning like. Ur dragging ppl on the TL within an inch of their life like say. Like say you don't have shit to be ashamed of. Like say you've never done shit wrong.

CLEO: What are you talking about?

KARA: Nothing man. Just leave it.

CLEO: Why are you moving so booky rn?

KARA: I said I wanna leave it man just chill.

TWITTERLUDE 6

▬▬▬▬▬▬▬
@▬▬▬▬▬▬

Ain't no way in hell this
@INCOGNEGRO squeaky clean!

06:16 AM · 5 Mar 2019

▬▬▬▬▬▬ @▬▬▬▬▬▬ · Mar 5
Truss me! I beg someone find this nigga dirty tweets.

▬▬▬ @▬▬▬▬▬▬ · Mar 5
Someone @ this b!

▬▬▬▬ @▬▬▬▬▬▬ · Mar 5
Twitter do ur thang!

Retweet   **Like**   **Follow**   **Like**

▬▬▬▬▬▬▬▬▬ @▬▬▬▬▬▬ · Mar 5
Mission accomplishedt!

INCOGNEGRO @INCOGNEGRO · Jun 6, 2014
Bum bye bye in a battybwoyyy head #tune

Retweet   **Retweet**   **Retweet**

IRL

CLEO: WTF tht's from before I changed my @
I s2g I fully don't remember saying that
And it's a Buju Banton song
My dad used to play it in the yard all the time
I was legit just quoting.

TWITTERLUDE 7

Yo @INCOGNEGRO acc
problematic AF! SMH!

06:17 AM - 5 Mar 2019

♡ ⟲ ♡ ✉

@ · Mar 5

And there's more...

 INCOGNEGRO @INCOGNEGRO · Mar 1, 2014
Lesbianz are acc disgusting,,,imagine licking poonani
#grim #nohomo 😤 😤 😤 😤 😤 😤 😤

♡ ⟲ ♡ ✉

IRL

CLEO:

Ewwwwwwwwwwwwwwwww
@INCOGNEGRO ain't nothing but a
GRADE A homophobe

06:21 AM - 5 Mar 2019

◯   ⇄   ♡   ✉

Retweet

Truss me zaddyyy she problematic af and have the cheek to try be
doing up social justice vigilante. Sis pleeeeeeeeeeeeeeeease.

◯   ⇄   ♡   ✉

When will y'all SJW learn tht the truth u hiding will always COME OUT
and it won't be pretty!!!

◯   ⇄   ♡   ✉

RETWEET
RETWEET
LIKE
FOLLOW
LIKE

IRL

CLEO: WTF! I can't believe this. Tht was time ago. And I. Yk me. I don't. I don't hate gay people. Queer people. I'm not –

KARA: You don't need to justify yourself to me. I'm not the TL.

CLEO: Wait what?

KARA: I'm js.

CLEO: Ur js what?

KARA: I'm js u seem to care a lot about how you're viewed on the TL.

CLEO: And?

KARA: Nvm.

CLEO: Ur not finished tho.

Pause.

KARA: It's just. U never talk about queer stuff on ur TL. And. U clearly. In the past. U…

CLEO: Ur not being srs? Dpmo. Ur siding w them when you kno me? When you acc kno my character irl? Ffs.

KARA: Well…yh…

CLEO: Yh what? Wtf is wrong w u rn? Come u use words. Ur a big woman bredrin. If you're implying I'm…I'm. That's just BS. Cah everyone said that typa shit in secondary – including u.

KARA:

CLEO: It's tru. U and I both know it's tru.

KARA: Whatever Cleo. Gwarn with your bad self. Ms Perfect Woke Queen.

CLEO:

KARA: Yo you're basically Angela Davis tbh. Sans licking poonani ofc.

CLEO: I'm not. I'm friends with u! And I mean. Not tht tht means.

KARA: I know what you mean. I know exactly what you mean.

TWITTERLUDE 9

███████████
@███████████

Ayyyyyyy I acc wanna know who
@INCOGNEGRO really be

06:28 AM - 5 Mar 2019

██████ @██████████ · Mar 5

Truss me zaddy!!!!!!!!! WTF is her real identity...

███████████ @█████████████ · Mar 5

She ain't gon' get away with this homophobia scott-free!

NOT ON MY WATCH   NOT ON MY WATCH

Retweet

████████████ @████████████ · Mar 5

(a la Rosie aka Tutty Gran) WE NEED JUSTICE! JUSTICE MI SEH!

███████████ @████████████ · Mar 5

I beg one of y'all Twitter sleuths do the damn thaaaaaaaaang!

#OUTINCOGNEGRO
#OUTINCOGNEGRO
#OUTINCOGNEGRO
#OUTINCOGNEGRO

IRL

KARA: U need to delete this account rn.

CLEO: Oh plsssss. I ain't deleting shit. How will the world-at-large succeeding to once again silence a helpless BW resolve to do anything?

KARA: F... F... S... Ur telling me you really can't see how you're at fault here?

CLEO: The only thing I've done is speak my truth!

KARA: R U ACC BEING SRS?

CLEO: Damn right bitch!

KARA: I acc can't w u rn.

CLEO: Well can bitch! Can w me! Cus as far as I can see the TL seem to think that dragging up historical dirty laundry will silence me. But NOT TODAY SATAN! Yo TL this is for you! I'M A BAD BITCH YOU CAN'T KILL MEH! CUS KING KONG AIN'T GOT SHIT ON ME AND I'MA CARRY ON WITH MY TWEETS. I'm a post another one. And another one...and... *(Ad infinitum.)*

62

KARA: Ur srsly gonna post another tweet?

CLEO: DAMN RIGHT!

TWITTERLUDE 10

INCOGNEGRO
@INCOGNEGRO

METHOD #6
#DEATHBYDISGRACE
This method doesn't involve death
at least not in the literal sense
But I want her to walk around like
one of those men
The men in top hats
Thick full red lips
Tap shoes
And skin black as tar
I want her to dress up as what she is

06:31 AM - 5 Mar 2019

INCOGNEGRO @INCOGNEGRO · Mar 5
I want her to have Aamito's lips and Hottentot Venus' hips
Without it being called a trend
I want her to be called blick in the playground
Drop lip
I want her to be whipped
And put in a box on show for a paying audience

INCOGNEGRO @INCOGNEGRO · Mar 5
I want her to replace her lip kits for cocoa butter or Vaseline
I want her thighs to be called fat not thick
Most of all I want her to come clean

64

INCOGNEGRO @INCOGNEGRO · Mar 5

I want her custom lace fronts to disintegrate into a no-lye relaxer and a hotcomb and I want her edges to get burnt
I want her boxer braids to turn into canerows and I want her to taste the salt tears that come into her eyes at 9
When she gets told she's not pretty enough for Cinderella
That's all I've got to tell her
Ms Jenner

♡ ⟲ ♡ ✉

INCOGNEGRO @INCOGNEGRO · Mar 5

I know you can keep up with the Kardashians
But can you keep up with me?
Miss Jenner I know you've got lips you like to overline but you've well and truly crossed the line this time
Because you are complicit in smudging Black women into oblivion
Do you know that?

♡ ⟲ ♡ ✉

IRL

KARA: Wtf is wrong with u rn! Look at urself honestly in the mirror and pree all your mistakes.

CLEO: *All* my mistakes?

KARA: I just – you've fucked up too Cleo. You have. And not just on the internet.

CLEO: BMT wtf r u talking about rn

KARA: Remember T'Sharn's 13th birthday party.

Beat.

Well just after. When we were lying on ur bed and you told me you were scared that no one was ever gonna love you and I said I love you. I love you. And then I was like I think I like girls and then I kissed you and you looked like you were gonna throw up and then you pushed me off and were like never ever say that ever again. So I didn't and I held that for a very very long time until one day it became too heavy to continue to hide. I think about that all the time. Having no one to run to. No one to tell. Not even my best friend. It shouldn't have been like that. It shouldn't have been like that Cleo. And it shouldn't have been so hard for me because you have no idea how hard it was. You have no fucking clue! You. You've fucked up too.

TWITTERLUDE 11

████████████
@████████████

Y'all WTF's the tea on @INCOGNEGRO true identity!

06:46 AM - 5 Mar 2019

◯   ⟲   ♡   ✉

████████████ @████████████ · Mar 5
Y'all look at what she RT'd last year

> ████████████ @████████████ · May 13, 2018
> Cleo Fuller elected Head of ACS

◯   ⟲   ♡   ✉

████████████ @████████████ · Mar 5
And the yr before that…

> ████████████ @████████████ · Jul 17, 2017
> Winner of full scholarship for first years commencing
> 2017...Cleo Fuller

◯   ⟲   ♡   ✉

████████████ @████████████ · Mar 5
Y'all I reversed her IP address @INCOGNEGRO defo dat bitch!!!!!!

◯   ⟲   ♡   ✉

████████████ @████████████ · Mar 5
😂😂😂😂😂😂😂😂😂😂😂😂😂

◯   ⟲   ♡   ✉

████████████ @████████████ · Mar 5
Y'ALL HACKER MFers are acc talented AF!

◯   ⟲   ♡   ✉

■■■■■■ @■■■■■■ · Mar 5

Truss me! Fiddy to anyone that can find out where she acc live!

💬　⟲　♡　✉

■■■■■■ @■■■■■■ · Mar 5

That would acc be sick!

💬　⟲　♡　✉

■■■■■■ @■■■■■■ · Mar 5

Yo @INCOGNEGRO we waiting on you @ the do'!

💬　⟲　♡　✉

Retweet　Report

■■■■■■ @■■■■■■ · Mar 5

YO @INCOGNEGRO = CLEO

💬　⟲　♡　✉

■■■■■■ @■■■■■■ · Mar 5

.@INCOGNEGRO = CLEO

💬　⟲　♡　✉

■■■■■■ @■■■■■■ · Mar 5

.@INCOGNEGRO = CLEO

💬　⟲　♡　✉

■■■■■■ @■■■■■■ · Mar 5

YOOOOOOOOOOOOOO Twitter done did they werqqqqqqqqqqqqqq
😂😂😂😂😂😂😂😂😂😂😂😂😂

💬　⟲　♡　✉

68

IRL

CLEO is silent. For tiiiiiiiiiiiiiiiiime.

KARA: Cleo with nothing to say. I never thought I'd see the day.

CLEO: BMT STFU.

KARA: Oh so now you wanna talk.

CLEO: I always knew tht u were an opp. I've known it from day.

KARA: Is this ur way of saying –

CLEO: – I'm not saying –

KARA: Of course ur not. Of course.

CLEO: Can u. Can u. Can u just fucking stop! Stop bringing old shit up!

KARA: Why? You do! All the time!

CLEO: It's not the same!

KARA: Yes it is. Why is it different for me? Cus u can't handle u f'd up? Tht y? Cus you can't handle wtf happened tht night.

CLEO: It's not that. I didn't realise. I didn't know you were being and I. And I –

KARA: Um what was that? Sounds like someone's stuttering. Stumbling over their own BS.

CLEO: Wtf! What about ur BS cah all now I ain't heard an apology for #wiggate!

KARA: We're talking about u fam! BMT STFU! And if u say fucking #wiggate one more time like say it's a political scandal I s2g I'ma fucking kill you!

CLEO: HAAAAAAAAAAAA! *(Monique voice.)* I would like to see it!

KARA: Oh pls you can't handle me b! And all I want is for you to admit when ur wrong.

CLEO: Wtf did I do that was soooooooooo wrong? Answer that for me one time pls. I tweeted two mildly problematic things so long ago I don't even remember them.

KARA: You still said it tho just like when we were on your bed and you said –

CLEO: You said I said –

KARA: You did.

CLEO: You said I said –

KARA: You did.

CLEO: Which I never would have said if I knew you acc were –

KARA: *am *are

CLEO: Yes. Are. Gay.

KARA: Queer. I identify as queer.

CLEO: Ok! KI! Queer. C now I cba to talk about it bcos idk what to say. I can't go back in time. If I could maybe I would. But I didn't know you were – are – even when you came out it was on the TL. I had no idea. You didn't tell me. I was shocked. I had to find out with every man and their mum. Did you ever think about how that made me feel? Huh? To see your new DP with a shaved head on some gay ass Britney 07 shit talmbout I've rejected heteronormative beauty standards because DUN DUN DUN. And when exactly were u planning on telling me?

KARA: I did.

CLEO: Tht time doesn't count.

KARA: Yh it do Cleo dpmo.

CLEO: Tbh I didn't kno u were being fr tht time.

KARA:

CLEO: Wyd???

KARA:

Mmmohmygod! Stop fucking lying!

CLEO: Kara stop it! Stfu.

KARA: I'm js.

CLEO: Ur acc wilding rn sis ffs.

KARA: Lol wtf ur the one wilin' rn sis tbh kmt.

CLEO: No u r!

KARA: LOOOOOOOOOOOOOOOOOOOOL TFW u kno you f'd up.

CLEO: LOOOOOOOOOOOOOOOOOOOOOOOOL TFW yk ur overreacting.

KARA: Oh gtfo! Tbh I'm done with this convo.

CLEO: *(À la Sweet Brown.)* Oh pls ain't nobody got time for you!

KARA: U know what I'm srsly done. Fr this time.

CLEO:

KARA: I'm being srs.

CLEO: Ite kl. Gtfo then.

KARA: Ite snm.

CLEO: Kl.

KARA: Bye Felicia.

CLEO: Girl, bye.

KARA:

CLEO: *(And suddenly vulnerable.)* Wait Kara wyd?

KARA: You are blocked from following @Kara and viewing her tweets.

CLEO: Stop airing me.

KARA: You are blocked from following @Kara and viewing her tweets.

CLEO: U acc blockdt me wtf!

KARA: You are blocked from following @Kara and viewing her tweets.

CLEO: Pls don't go I need u rn! Pls!

KARA: You are blocked from following @Kara and viewing her tweets.

And suddenly CLEO or @INCOGNEGRO realises she is alone. Summoning her last iota of courage she enters the TL again. As her identity is exposed, she is rendered hypervisible. This might mean a blinding light is shone on her.

@INCOGNEGRO tweets.

 INCOGNEGRO
@INCOGNEGRO

I'm @INCOGNEGRO a.k.a Cleo.
Well my real name is acc just
Cleo. Whatever real is anyway idk
anymore tbh

07:02 AM - 5 Mar 2019

♡   ⟲   ♡   ✉

INCOGNEGRO @INCOGNEGRO · Mar 5

I just wanted to say something about my twitter page and the shit I've posted on the TL of past and of late

♡ ⭯ ♡ ✉

INCOGNEGRO @INCOGNEGRO · Mar 5

I wanna apologise for the two homophobic tweets I posted in 2014.

♡ ⭯ ♡ ✉

INCOGNEGRO @INCOGNEGRO · Mar 5

It wasn't kl or funny and I take full responsibility for my actions. I now understand that both those tweets even to this day are inherently problematic + harmful

♡ ⭯ ♡ ✉

INCOGNEGRO @INCOGNEGRO · Mar 5

Also I have never ever set out to, nor do I intend to in the immediate or extended future acc kill Kylie Jenner, the comments were merely made in jest to wittily dissect the former's right to her empire, sphere of influence and monetary income

♡ ⭯ ♡ ✉

INCOGNEGRO @INCOGNEGRO · Mar 5

So pls pls pls don't try and find my acc address I beg you pls srsly

♡ ⭯ ♡ ✉

Over the course of the following, Cleo @INCOGNEGRO goes into heartspeak. Her two heretofore separate identities as the IRL Cleo and TL @INCOGNEGRO conspire to cross over and become one as she allows the truth to pour from her. As she does so, she expands and swells in the space. In doing all of the above, she breaks the form of Twitter and eventually the internet itself...

INCOGNEGRO
@INCOGNEGRO

I really struggle with how to say these things
and I don't wanna look angry and cry

74

and sometimes I'm scared it will make me look crazy if I get angry
and cry
and no one will listen to me or ppl will just think I'm weak or just
a mewling girl or some old archaic female stereotype which might
not apply to me anyway bcos I'm a black woman and sometimes
people don't really see me as a woman anyway

or as much of a woman

or even human

and that makes me really fucking angry

hate to fulfil the stereotype or

trope

but sometimes that's all you can do

.

there you go

maybe it's fucked up

maybe I'm fucked up because that shouldn't be the only thing I
want as a woman

to be beautiful

to be considered beautiful

but I do

And actually I don't think that's fucked up

I think that's okay

I think it should be okay to want to be looked at and seen as
beautiful

but maybe I've been doing it in the wrong way

Doing it for someone

Rather than for myself

but I don't know if there's any other way to see myself apart from
in reference to someone else

cus like every time I think about my childhood these memories just
come up of things I didn't realise were fucked up or didn't realise
what they meant at the time like

these words being flung about like fishy or droplip and they
weren't terms of endearment or compliments

they were cusses straight out ways to make people like me, little
black children, little black girls feel like shit

Feel ugly

Because of the size of their lips...

so when I was 16 and I saw Kylie's new lips I couldn't help but feel

Can't help but feel

A sense of...indignation

No more than that

I can't help but feel a sense that I want to punch her lights out

That if I watched her suffer

If I watched her die

There's a tiny bit of me that would maybe rejoice

Or maybe not rejoice

But just

Stand there for a minute and look

And you know maybe even smile

Maybe just

Maybe even finish her off myself…

You know what

I'm watering myself down

I have thought of fucking killing her

Otherwise this

I wouldn't have tweeted any of this shit in the first place

Pause.

Am I violent?

.

.

.

METHOD #7
#DEATHBYDISPLACEMENT

.

I can't help but think about her
Being disgraced
Being dragged from her home across the Atlantic
Age: 21
And put in a cage

Paraded and pimped in a peep-show for a paying audience
And poked
Prodded
Displaced
Placed next to livestock
On a block
For people to watch for decades
Until
Her body was exhausted of interest
forced into the streets with nothing to eat
Seduced into sex work
Fucked senseless
Infected with syphilis
Then left to die until her body decayed
How even in death her body was defaced
Her corpse stolen
Sold on as a specimen to scientists
Degraded in daguerreotypes
And eventually dismantled
Her corpse kept as a prototype
How her cadaver was placed on a chain
Between monkeys and men
Then
Preserved in a plaster cast
Her coil relegated into a relic for
Anatomists
Pseudoscientists
Who analysed
Dissected
And reflected on her full form
Then
Carved her up like a continent
Her genitals and brains jellied in jars
And the rest of her remains left in an open grave
On public display
For all to look upon
Her buxom busty form
Being mocked and mimicked for centuries
Even to this day
And that woman's name wasn't Kylie
She was known as Saartjie…

Sara…

Ssehura…

Hottentot…

I don't even know her name

History failed to record it.

She was a Black South African woman in the 18th century

Who had exactly the same body

The same features

And didn't receive a fucking penny

Now remember her story.

Tweets from the Twittersphere begin to reach fever pitch.

Remember her story!

Remember her story!

Remember her story!

The Twittersphere completely explodes.

The Twittersphere completely
The Twittersphere completely
The Twittersphere completely
The Twittersphere completely
The Twittersphere completely
The Twittersphere completely
The Twittersphere complet

THE POST-MORTEM

CLEO and KARA stand still facing each other.

Debris from the Twittersphere fills the stage. CLEO is sat stunned. KARA is looking at her.

KARA: .

CLEO: .

KARA: .

CLEO: .

KARA: Um. Are you

CLEO: .

KARA: alright?

> *CLEO bursts into tears. Like she might never stop.*

CLEO: I'm just so exhausted.

> *Pause.*

> And I'm tired of explaining why. Giving a reason for every bit of my rage. My pain. And it's like all I can feel is weight. Dragging me down. All the time. Every fucking day. When I wake up. When I go to sleep. And I…I just don't wanna feel heavy no more.

KARA: You don't have to…we don't have to.

CLEO: It feels like it. Like we ain't got a choice.

KARA: She didn't. Saartjie. But Cleo we do. We *can* move. We can leave shit behind.

CLEO: Doesn't feel like it.

> *Beat.*

KARA: I have an idea.

Some time has passed. CLEO and KARA drag something ressembling a body onto the platform. They open the traps and throw it in. Cover it with earth. Suddenly they stop, standing over it.

CLEO: Rah this shit is heavy.

KARA: 'Course it is. It's all our trauma.

CLEO: I mean it's a duvet with a couple old wigs –

KARA: – It's what it represents. Things that oppress us. Weigh us down. This is for all the wxmen that were denied a right to a voice. To expression. All the black womxn…black femmes denied their right to just…be. It's for Saartjie and all the other nameless, faceless black womxn who were told they weren't really womxn. Subjected to a gaze. Weighed down. It's for they and them. Us.

KARA picks up some earth. Sprinkles it over the sacrifice.

CLEO joins her.

KARA: Earth. *(Referencing the park.)* Air. *(She produces a zoot and lighter, lights the spliff.)* Fire.

She passes the zoot to CLEO.

CLEO: Nah I'm good.

KARA: Come on. Just this once. They go low. We get highhhhhhhhh.

CLEO: You know I don't do weed.

KARA: You don't do regular weed. But this spliff is special. This right here. This is a… *diasporic* zoot. This shit's spiritual. And she's begging for you to partake.

Beat.

KARA drags on the zoot then passes, smiling. CLEO concedes and proceeds to take a drag off the zoot.

As they get high, the whole room might go dark. She, with significant sauce and significant flair, takes a drag from the zoot.

80

*It's loooooooooooooud. Something in the room changes. She passes
it to CLEO. CLEO tries to take a drag, dissolving into coughs.*

KARA: What. The. Fuck!

CLEO: What?

KARA: You're telling me you can't feel that?

CLEO: …no…

KARA: You did inhale, right?

CLEO: …yeah…

KARA demonstrates what she means with the zoot.

*CLEO, with significantly less flair and significantly less sauce, attempts
to replicate.*

CLEO: *(Seeing the light.)* Faaaaaaaaaaaaaaaaaam.

KARA: Hold my hand.

CLEO does.

*As the passion takes both of them, they move. Ancestral. Spiritual.
Magic. Black girl magic-ish. An echo of something. Or maybe they're
just high as fuck. They scream together in shock at what they both
feel. Joyful. Glorious. They continue to move at the peak of the high.*

Then.

The chill of a spirit passing through.

CLEO: Saartjie?

Pause.

I praise you for helping me to break out
the boxes I stand in
Helping me to break free
Your power
Your rage
Welling inside of me
Your spirit suspending my soul

Your strength making me feel completely whole
Like I don't need another half
To validate my beauty
Like I can transcend the need for romantic company
Got me feeling like I can be anything I wanna be
Like if I really wanna be
I can just be a massive motherfucking shadow that
whispers MENARETRASH over men's shoulders
That follows them in cars at night and blinds their eyes
with LED headlights
Like if I wanted to
if I really wanted to
I could swallow all of them completely
whole
Saartjie
I praise you for letting me know my body is mine
all the time
I praise you
Allowing me to tear down every caricature
construction
conception
of black woman that has ever been
That has ever been seen
Saartjie
I praise you for making me feel like a true fucking queen
Not in the
Colonial
Capitalist
hegemony
But my own definition of royalty
Where I can create my own freedom
Kingdom
Crown
A place where I'm always on top
And I never have to come down!

Then in an instant, Saartjie's spirit disappears.

*And as soon as it began...it is over. And whatever it was...is gone.
They stop and touch their heads. They close the trap.*

CLEO: Rahtid that shit's strong!

82

KARA: Trust me!

CLEO: Are my eyes supposed to feel like this?

KARA: Yeah fam just chill.

CLEO: I am never smoking weed again!

KARA: Ay real talk have you got any crips on you?

CLEO: Why would I have *crisps* on me?

KARA: Come we go shop.

CLEO: It's cold. I want my bed.

KARA: I'll be quick! I promise

CLEO: Oh my daze…

> *They start to leave. Then seemingly out of nowhere CLEO stops.*

CLEO: I'm not gonna lie I'm feeling very paro right now.

KARA: Cleo chill it's perfectly normal post-spliff.

CLEO: Nah I really don't think it's that man. I. It's like the weight before
– but worse. Like I'm being watched or something.

KARA: What…like now?

> *Suddenly KARA and CLEO see the spectators watching. This might
> mean the house lights coming up. Whatever it means, this moment
> should take as long as it needs to take to land.*

> *Silence.*

CLEO: They're just sat there not saying jack.

KARA: What are you gonna do now…clap?

END OF PLAY

AN AFTERTHOUGHT

Saartjie, or Sarah Baartman as she became later known, was a South African woman born in the Eastern Cape in 1789. After being transported as a curiosity throughout Europe during the late 18th and early 19th century, she died at the tender age of 26 due to unknown causes. In death, her body was put on display at France's Musée de l'Homme until 1974. On 9 August 2002, after a series of requests from Nelson Mandela, her remains were successfully repatriated to South Africa and buried in Hankey in the Eastern Cape.

If you are interested in learning more about Saartjie Baartman's story, I'd highly recommend *Representation and Black Womanhood: The Legacy of Sarah Baartman* (2015), an essay anthology collated by Natasha Gordon-Chipembere, a book which greatly inspired and influenced this play.

BIBLIOGRAPHY

*A bibliography, to the best of my knowledge, of all the memes,
gifs and Twitter references made in the play, lest our labour
and records be swept away again…*

In order of appearance in the text:

Black woman slow clapping, GIF, woman unknown, source unknown

Affronted black girl, GIF, Marsai Martin as Diane Johnson, *Black-ish*

Shocked black man, GIF, Titus Burgess as Titus Andromedon,
The Unbreakable Kimmy Schmidt

watisdemeaningofalldisjackie, Saying, Person unknown, *Cheaters*

Black woman shooting, GIF, Queen Latifah as Cleo, *Set It Off*

Black woman laughing with glass of wine, GIF, Tiffany Pollard

Black woman swindling knife, GIF, Tiffany Pollard

Unbothered Black woman, GIF, Person unknown, source unknown

And I oop, GIF, Jasmine Masters, *Jasmine Masters handle your liquor*
(Youtube)

Get out of my Caucasian home, GIF and vine, Branden Miller as
Joanne The Scammer

U ready to fucking die! I'm a bad bitch you can't kill meh!, saying and
originally a vine, people unknown

The ting go skraaaa, Youtube clip and song, Big Shaq – 'Man's Not Hot'

KING KONG AIN'T GOT SHIT ON ME!, film clip, Denzel Washington
as Alonzo Harris in *Training Day*

Black woman sliding off sofa, GIF, Tiffany Pollard, source unknown

Black woman emerging from car set on fire, GIF, Angela Bassett as
Bernadine Harris in *Waiting to Exhale*

Kermit drinking tea, meme, source unknown

Brown cartoon fist, meme, *Arthur*

Black girl with open palm, meme, Keisha Johnson

Black woman rolling eyes with mobile, GIF, Nene Leakes, *The Real
Housewives of Atlanta*

Black guy with outstretched lips, meme and GIF, Conceited

Black guy with crossed arms, Y'all finished or y'all done?, meme and saying, *Birdman*, *The Breakfast Club*

I cannot see I'm legally blind!, meme and saying, Donna Goudeau

Black woman nodding and holding back tears, GIF, Oprah Winfrey, *The Oprah Winfrey Show*

Black guy in realisation, GIF, Wee-bey, *The Wire*

Reclaiming my time! Reclaiming my time!, saying and video, Maxine Waters

Black woman picking up her bag and leaving, GIF, Viola Davis as Annalise Keating, *How To Get Away With Murder*

Black man eating popcorn, GIF, Michael Jackson, *Thriller*

How sway!, GIF and saying, Kanye West, *Sway in The Morning*

Why the fuck you lying?, vine and music video, Nicholas Fraser

Real friends, how many of us, song, Kanye West, 'Real Friends', *The Life of Pablo*

Another one! Another one!, GIF and saying, DJ Khaled

Black woman with glasses rolling eyes, Tamar Braxton, *The Real*

Black woman expressing disgust on her face, Clare Perkins, source unknown

Not on my watch!, Iyanla Vanzant on *Iyanla: Fix My Life!*

We need justice!, Rosie Bailey

I said what I said!, Nene Leakes, *The Real Housewives of Atlanta*

I would like to see it, M'Onique, *The Steve Harvey Show*

I was waiting on you at the do' with neck snap, Ms Foxy, *Beyond Scared Straight*

Disappearing black boy, GIF and vine, Nileseyy Niles

For a complete listing of
Methuen Drama titles, visit:
www.bloomsbury.com/drama

Follow us on Twitter and keep up to date
with our news and publications
@MethuenDrama